Wake me up
when I'm a size 5

**Other Cathy books
from Andrews and McMeel**

Thin thighs in thirty years

Men should come with instruction booklets

A mouthful of breath mints and no one to kiss

Another Saturday night of wild and reckless abandon

A hand to hold, an opinion to reject

Why do the right words always come out of the wrong
mouth?

Wake me up
when I'm a size 5

A cathy Collection
by Cathy Guisewite

Andrews and McMeel
A Universal Press Syndicate Company
Kansas City • New York

ISBN: 0-8362-2069-2

Library of Congress Catalog Card Number: 85-61452

First Printing, July 1985
Fifth Printing, January 1989

5

NO! DON'T DO IT! DON'T CALL HIM! NO!!

"NO" BECAUSE IT'S WRONG TO CALL, OR "NO" BECAUSE I'M SCARED TO CALL?

"NO" BECAUSE HE MIGHT HATE ME, OR "NO" BECAUSE HE MIGHT LOVE ME? OR "NO" BECAUSE IT JUST ISN'T RIGHT?

WHY DIDN'T YOU CALL HIM, CATHY?

I DON'T KNOW. I CAN'T TELL MY CONSCIENCE FROM MY INSECURITIES.

HERE'S OUR CARD FOR THEM... "CONGRATULATIONS. LOVE, CATHY AND IRVING."

I NEVER SAW "CATHY AND IRVING" WRITTEN TOGETHER LIKE THAT.

WHEN PEOPLE START SIGNING BOTH NAMES ON GREETING CARDS, IT SOUNDS SO SERIOUS! IT SOUNDS LIKE WE'RE A REAL "COUPLE."

I'M NOT READY FOR THAT! I'M NOT READY FOR US TO BE LABELED IN PRINT AS A "COUPLE"!!!

MEN GET SO EMOTIONAL AT WEDDINGS.

I WILL NEVER GO TO ANOTHER WEDDING WHILE I'M SINGLE!!

I WILL NEVER AGAIN TAKE A DATE TO A WEDDING! I WILL NEVER AGAIN BUY A NEW OUTFIT FOR A WEDDING, JUST IN CASE THE USHERS ARE CUTER THAN MY DATE!!

AND LAST, I WILL NEVER AGAIN SPEND MY ELECTRIC BILL MONEY ON A WEDDING GIFT FOR A WOMAN WHOSE NEW HUSBAND EARNS $60,000 MORE THAN I DO!!

SINGLE PEOPLE HAVE OUR OWN WEDDING VOWS.

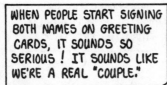

DO YOU THINK HIS NOSE IS REALLY THIS BIG, OR THAT THE LIGHTING IS JUST BAD IN THE PICTURE?

CATHY, THIS IS THE FINAL RESPONDENT FROM THE PERSONAL AD YOU RAN.

YOU SWORE YOU'D HAVE A BRIGHT, POSITIVE ATTITUDE!

A BRIGHT, POSITIVE ATTITUDE!

IF HE REALLY LOVES YOU, MAYBE HE'LL GET A NOSE JOB.

YOU'RE EVEN PRETTIER THAN YOU SOUNDED ON THE PHONE, AND I THOUGHT YOU WERE GORGEOUS ON THE PHONE.

AHEM... UM... THANK YOU. COME IN.

I DON'T MEAN TO SOUND LIKE I'M SO INTO LOOKS... I'M HERE BECAUSE I ADMIRED THE SENSITIVITY IN THE AD YOU WROTE.

AHEM... UM...I.. HEE HEE.. AHEM...

I THINK YOU'RE A REMARKABLE WOMAN FOR TAKING CONTROL OF YOUR SOCIAL LIFE.

UM... HEE HEE HEE AHEM UM HEE HEE HEE

ARE YOU FLIRTING OR CHOKING TO DEATH?

I'M SO ATTRACTED TO THIS MAN...PLEASE DON'T LET HIM BE DIVORCED.

I SHOULD TELL YOU, CATHY... I'M DIVORCED.

PLEASE...NO HOSTILITIES WITH THE EX-WIFE.

I STILL HAVE REAL PROBLEMS WITH MY EX-WIFE.

OH, PLEASE, PLEASE, PLEASE... ...NO SMALL CHILDREN!!

WE HAVE TWO SMALL CHILDREN.

WHAT DO YOU THINK OF PAUL?

HE'S EVERYTHING I IMAGINED.

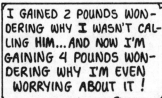

"ALL FINISHED?"

"YES. THE BATHING SUITS THAT ARE AN INSULT TO ALL OF WOMANHOOD ARE WADDED UP IN THE CORNER."

"THE BATHING SUITS THAT MIGHT LOOK OKAY ON SOME WOMEN, BUT MAKE ME PERSONALLY LOOK LIKE A COW, ARE PILED ON THE CHAIR."

"THE SUITS THAT WEREN'T PERFECT, BUT FLATTERED PARTS OF ME, ARE NEATLY RE-HUNG ON THEIR LITTLE HANGERS."

"WE'RE NICER TO THOSE WHO ARE KIND TO US."

FITTING ROOMS

1

"PAUL IS DIVORCED WITH 2 LITTLE KIDS, MOM, BUT I DON'T THINK WE SHOULD MENTION THIS TO DAD."

"AHEM... UM... DIVORCED? AHEM... 2...2 LITTLE KIDS??"

"I DON'T THINK DAD COULD HANDLE IT LIKE YOU CAN."

"HOO BOY! NO. YOUR FATHER IS NOT READY FOR THIS ONE!"

"DAD JUST ISN'T AS OPEN-MINDED. THIS WILL BE OUR LITTLE SECRET."

"OUR LITTLE SECRET."

GAIN A CONFIDENCE, SACRIFICE A REACTION.

"OF COURSE YOU CAN BRING YOUR KIDS OVER, PAUL! I'M WONDERFUL WITH CHILDREN!"

"REALLY, CATHY?"

"I'VE ALWAYS HAD STRONG MOTHERING INSTINCTS! I LOVE TO FEED... TO NURTURE... TO HELP LITTLE LIVES GROW!!"

HALLELUJAH.

11

WHEN CATHY COMES IN THE DOOR, PRETEND NOTHING'S GOING ON.

RIGHT. NOTHING'S GOING ON.

THEN I'LL LEAP OUT AND ASK HER ABOUT HER DATE WITH PAUL AND HIS KIDS!

THEN I'LL RUN IN AND GRILL HER ABOUT WHAT HAPPENED TO IRVING!!

THEN WE'LL BOTH JUMP UP AND DOWN AND OFFER OUR OPINIONS!!

HI. WHAT'S GOING ON?

WE'RE PLANNING A SURPRISE PARTY FOR OUR DAUGHTER.

I WROTE A 20-PAGE MASTERPIECE ON THE BLAKE DEAL. NO ONE NOTICED.

CHARLENE

I SINGLE-HANDEDLY SAVED THE WILEY ACCOUNT. NO ONE NOTICED.

CHARLENE

WHY IS IT THAT WHEN I HAVE ONE LITTLE DATE WITH A MAN AND HIS TWO CHILDREN, THE ENTIRE OFFICE SUDDENLY KNOWS EVERY DETAIL?!!

CHARLENE

YOU TOLD EVERYONE, CATHY.

AH.

ARLENE

HOW WAS THE BIG DATE WITH PAUL AND HIS KIDS, CATHY?

ELEVEN STRAIGHT HOURS OF WHIMPERING, WHINING, SULKING, CLINGING, PETTY JEALOUSIES AND TEMPER TANTRUMS.

KIDS THAT AGE ARE ALWAYS A LOT TO HANDLE.

I WASN'T TALKING ABOUT THE KIDS. I WAS TALKING ABOUT ME.

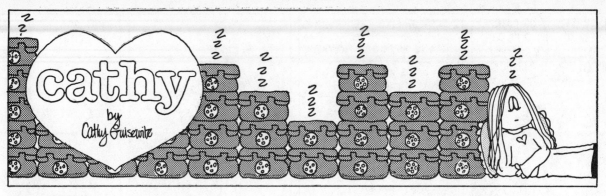

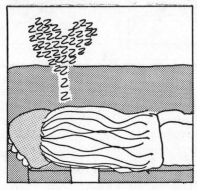

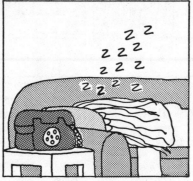

...HMPG?

HI, CATHY. IT'S IRVING. ARE YOU ASLEEP?

....HUH?..IRGVL??.. ...NO... NO, I'M NOT SLEEGF...

YOU SOUND LIKE YOU'RE ASLEEP.

...HUH?....NO...WAIT.. ...AHEM!...NO, NO I'M NOT ASLEEP.

SLAP SLAP!

IF YOU'RE ASLEEP, I'LL CALL ANOTHER TIME.

NO..WAIT. I'M AWAKE..WAIT! I'M AWAKE!

SLAP SLAP!

SPLASH!

JOG JOG

JOG JOG

WELL, I JUST WANTED TO SAY HI. SEE YOU TOMORROW....

WAIT! I'M AWAKE! I'M FULLY....

CLICK!

16

TO GRANT, WHO LEFT ME WITH 12 IRATE CLIENTS TO CONSOLE WHILE HE'S SCUBA DIVING IN THE CARIBBEAN.

TO SUSAN, WHO BEGGED ME TO SORT OUT HER 300-PAGE MARKETING FIASCO WHILE SHE'S WINDSURFING IN HAWAII.

TO MORRIE, WHO ASKED ME TO "WATCH OVER $2,000,000 OF BUSINESS" WHILE HE'S DRIFTING THROUGH ITALY ON A RIVERBOAT.

I ALWAYS GAIN WEIGHT ON VACATIONS.

ATTENTION ALL EMPLOYEES: COPIES OF "WHAT WAS SAID ABOUT YOU WHILE YOU WERE ON VACATION" ARE NOW AVAILABLE AT THE RECEPTION DESK FOR $9.95.

FOR AN ADDITIONAL $4.95, YOU MAY OBTAIN A LIST OF WHO SNOOPED THROUGH YOUR DESK WHILE YOU WERE GONE. IF YOU HAVEN'T HAD YOUR VACATION YET AND WANT A PRE-...

BAM RIP RIP CRASH RIP

I LOVE AN OFFICE WITH AN OPEN MIND TOWARD FREE-LANCING.

IRVING SAYS HE WANTS ME BACK. IF I COME BACK, HE'LL LEAVE.

IRVING'S PLEADING WITH ME TO BE "HIS" AGAIN. AS SOON AS I'M "HIS," HE'LL TAKE OFF.

IRVING, SWEETIE, I'M BACK!! I'M ALL YOURS!

AAACK! WAIT... WAIT... AAACK!

NEVER MIND. I WAS JUST CALLING TO CONFIRM YOUR FLIGHT.

19

MY BIOLOGICAL CLOCK SAYS IT'S TIME TO HAVE CHILDREN. MY EMOTIONAL CLOCK SAYS KIDS CAN WAIT...IT'S TIME FOR A SOLID RELATIONSHIP!

MY PSYCHOLOGICAL CLOCK SAYS THE RELATIONSHIP CAN WAIT...IT'S TIME TO GET MY CAREER UNDER CONTROL!

MY PHYSIOLOGICAL CLOCK SAYS MY CAREER WILL GO RIGHT DOWN THE DRAIN IF I DON'T GET OUT OF HERE... IT'S TIME FOR A VACATION !!

I HAVE JET LAG FROM FOUR PLACES, AND I DIDN'T EVEN GO ANYWHERE YET.

YOU CAN'T TAKE YOUR VACATION THIS MONTH, CATHY. WE HAVE A CRISIS ON THE THORNTON PROJECT.

I WAS ROBBED OF MY VACATION LAST YEAR BECAUSE OF A CRISIS ON THE THORNTON PROJECT, MR. PINKLEY.

IN FACT, THIS IS THE EXACT SAME CRISIS !! DO YOU ACTUALLY EXPECT ME TO MISS MY VACATION TWO YEARS IN A ROW FOR THE EXACT SAME CRISIS ?!!

YOUNG PEOPLE HAVE NO SENSE OF CORPORATE TRADITION.

WHERE ARE YOU GOING ON YOUR VACATION, CATHY ?

I WANT TO GO SOMEWHERE I'VE NEVER BEEN BEFORE, MOM.

I WANT TO SEARCH FOR BURIED TREASURES...EXPLORE LOST FRONTIERS...

...REDISCOVER THE MYSTERY AND ROMANCE OF ANOTHER TIME !!

WHY DON'T YOU SPEND THE WEEK CLEANING OUT YOUR STORAGE ROOM ?

VERY FUNNY, MOTHER.

YOU'RE TERRIFIED OF GETTING CLOSE, AND YOU'LL NEVER CHANGE, IRVING.

I NEED SOMEONE I CAN **PLAN** WITH. I WANT A LONG-RANGE, LONG-TERM, LIFETIME RELATIONSHIP!

LET'S TAKE OUR VACATION TOGETHER THIS YEAR, CATHY, AND SEE HOW IT WORKS.

ARE YOU CRAZY?!! I'M NOT READY FOR THAT BIG OF A COMMITMENT!

AREN'T YOU TRYING TO LOSE WEIGHT BEFORE VACATION, CATHY?

NO. I WANT TO BE AS FAT AS POSSIBLE BEFORE I LEAVE SO I CAN MAKE A DRAMATIC ENTRANCE WHEN I GET BACK.

DON'T YOU WANT TO GET A HEAD START ON YOUR TAN??

NO. I WANT TO LEAVE TOTALLY PALE SO I'LL LOOK MORE TAN WHEN I GET BACK.

I WILL STAY INDOORS, EAT, AND LOOK SLOPPY, SO WHEN I COME HOME I'LL LOOK THIN, TAN AND GORGEOUS!!

I'M DOING MORE TO PLAN MY RETURN THAN I AM TO PLAN MY TRIP.

WHEN I ASKED YOU TO TAKE A VACATION WITH ME, YOU SCREAMED AT ME, CATHY.

I THOUGHT YOU WERE JOKING, IRVING.

WHY WOULD YOU THINK I WAS JOKING?

ANY TIME YOU SAY SOMETHING SERIOUS ABOUT US, I THINK YOU'RE JOKING.

I ONLY **ACT** LIKE I'M JOKING BECAUSE **YOU** ACT LIKE I'M JOKING!!

I ONLY ACT LIKE YOU'RE JOKING BECAUSE YOU **SOUND** LIKE YOU'RE JOKING!!

WE WANT TO TAKE A VACATION TOGETHER.

YOU MUST BE JOKING.

21

WHAT'S IN THE BOX??

JUST SOME OLD CLOTHES I'M GETTING RID OF.

MIND IF I TAKE A PEEK?

WHAT'S THIS NICE SWEATER DOING IN YOUR "GET-RID-OF" BOX, CATHY?

IT HAS A BIG SPOT THAT WON'T COME OUT, MOM. IT'S RUINED.

NONSENSE. WE CAN JUST DYE THE REST OF THE SWEATER TO MATCH THE SPOT!

TRUST ME, MOM. IT'S RUINED.

...WHEN THE DYE FAILS, WE CAN TRY DUPLICATING THE SPOT TO CREATE A CUTE "SPOT PATTERN."

...WHEN THE SPOT PATTERN FAILS, WE CAN JUST CUT OUT THE SPOTS AND INSERT COLORFUL FABRIC... ...WHEN THE FABRIC PLAN FAILS, WE SIMPLY EMBROIDER OVER.....

....THERE! NOW IT'S RUINED!!

YOU YOUNG PEOPLE ALWAYS LOOK FOR THE SHORTCUTS TO EVERYTHING.

OF COURSE IRVING AND I AREN'T JUST GOING ON VACATION TOGETHER, MOM. WE'LL BE WITH A WHOLE GROUP.

A GROUP. OH, SURE.

OKAY, IT ISN'T EXACTLY A GROUP, BUT WE'LL BE VISITING IRVING'S RELATIVES.

RELATIVES. GIVE ME A BREAK.

OKAY, WE WON'T ACTUALLY SEE RELATIVES, BUT WE'LL BE STAYING WITH A LOVELY OLDER COUPLE WHO HAVE TWO SPARE GUEST ROOMS.

OUR PRAYERS HAVE BEEN ANSWERED, DEAR! SHE CAME UP WITH A LIE WE CAN BELIEVE!

WE CAN'T GO ON THE AIRLINE YOU PICKED, SWEETIE. I'M NOT ON THEIR MILEAGE PROGRAM.

...WAIT. WE CAN'T RENT OUR CAR FROM THEM. I GET BONUS POINTS WITH ANOTHER COMPANY.

WE CAN'T STAY AT THAT HOTEL. I DON'T GET ANY EXTRA POINTS THERE.

WHICH WOULD YOU RATHER DO, TRAVEL WITH ME OR PICK UP 6,000 MILEAGE POINTS?!

AH. THE ROMANCE OF TRAVEL.

I OVERSLEPT. THEN I GOT UP AND OVERATE.

THEN I RACED AROUND PANICKING ABOUT EVERYTHING I WANTED TO DO TODAY.

NOW I'M GOING TO SIT DOWN AND PRETEND TO TAKE CARE OF MY CORRESPONDENCE.

I'M PRACTICING FOR MY VACATION.

UM...HELLO. IT'S US AGAIN.

NO PROBLEM.

YOUR TRAVEL

OUR STAFF IS HAVING A RAFFLE BASED ON HOW MANY MORE TIMES YOU TWO CHANGE YOUR ITINERARY IN THE NEXT THREE DAYS.

GRAND PRIZE GOES TO THE AGENT WHO COMES CLOSEST TO GUESSING THE EXACT HOUR YOU'LL GET INTO A FIGHT AND CANCEL THE WHOLE VACATION!

THIS IS INCREDIBLE.

I KNOW. NOT MANY AGENCIES WOULD HAVE THE ENTIRE OFFICE ROOTING FOR YOU.

WE SPENT THE '60s PHILOSO-PHIZING, SCRUTINIZING AND **ACTUALIZING**, ANDREA.

WE SPENT THE '70s INTEL-LECTUALIZING, ANALYZING AND **VERBALIZING**.

NOW IT'S THE '80s AND YOU'RE TAKING A TRIP WITH IRVING TO **VALIDATE** YOUR PERSONAL GROWTH IN A ONE-TO-ONE INTERACTION!!

I WAS JUST LOOKING FOR-WARD TO FINALLY GETTING TO DO SOMETHING STUPID.

PICTURES OF HOW HAPPY MY PARENTS LOOKED BEFORE I TOLD THEM I WAS TAKING THIS VACATION WITH IRVING...

PHONE NUMBERS OF RELATIVES WHO LIVE IN STATES I'M FLY-ING RIGHT OVER....ADDRESSES OF FRIENDS I'VE IGNORED...

PROJECTS THAT COULD HAVE MADE ME RICH IF I'D FIN-ISHED THEM...BOOKS THAT COULD HAVE CHANGED MY LIFE IF I'D READ THEM....

ALL SET, CATHY?

MY SUITCASE IS READY. I'M JUST PACKING MY EMO-TIONAL BAGGAGE.

HAWAII. HI, MOM. CATHY AND I ARE GOING ON VACATION TO HAWAII.

OLDER COUPLE. TWO SPARE GUEST-ROOMS.

WE'RE STAYING WITH A NICE OLDER COUPLE WITH TWO SPARE GUESTROOMS.

MESSAGES RELAYED THROUGH ANDREA.

THEIR PHONE IS BROKEN, BUT ANDREA CAN GET MESSAGES TO US IF NECESSARY.

WE'RE SYNCHRONIZING OUR MOTHERS.

IRVING... LISTEN! THERE ARE NO CRYING BABIES ON THIS AIRPLANE!

IT'S GOING TO BE A WONDERFUL, ROMANTIC FLIGHT!

I'M SO HAPPY TO BE WITH YOU, CATHY!

WE ARE THE LUCKIEST TWO PEOPLE IN THE WORLD TO BE WITH EACH OTHER ON THIS ROMANTIC, QUIET FLIGHT!!

WAAAAHH!

WHY ARE YOU LEAPING UP TO GET OFF THE PLANE? THERE ARE 300 PEOPLE AHEAD OF US.

I'M THE TYPE WHO LIKES TO LEAP UP, IRVING.

YOU CAN'T GO ANYWHERE, CATHY.

I LIKE TO LEAP UP JUST IN CASE.

YOU MIGHT NOT GO ANYWHERE IF YOU LEAP UP, IRVING, BUT IF YOU DON'T LEAP UP YOU DEFINITELY WON'T GO ANYWHERE!!!

WILL EVERYONE SIT DOWN?! WE'RE NOT AT THE GATE YET!!

LEADERS GET USED TO A CERTAIN AMOUNT OF RIDICULE.

27

WE'VE BEEN ON VACATION FOR 3 DAYS. WHY HASN'T CATHY HIT ME WITH "THE RELATIONSHIP DISCUSSION" YET ???

SHE'S TORTURING ME ON PURPOSE! SHE'S WAITING UNTIL I'M RELAXED SO SHE CAN MAKE IT A SNEAK ATTACK!!

WHAT'S THE MATTER WITH ME? CATHY DOESN'T THINK LIKE THAT! I SHOULD BE SO GRATEFUL TO BE WITH A WOMAN LIKE CATHY!

...5..4...3...2....

THAT'S CATHY CALLING FROM HAWAII!

WAIT! IF WE ANSWER ON THE FIRST RING SHE'LL THINK WE'RE JUST SITTING HERE WAITING TO POUNCE ON THE PHONE.

RING!

IF WE ANSWER AFTER TWO RINGS SHE'LL THINK WE'RE SITTING HERE WAITING TO POUNCE, BUT WE'RE TRYING TO ACT BLASÉ ABOUT IT.

RING RING

FOUR RINGS IS THE PERFECT AMOUNT! FOUR RINGS LETS US BE DESPERATE WITH DIGNITY!

RING

NOT ALL PARENTS GET TO KEEP USING THEIR DATING SKILLS THIS FAR INTO THE MARRIAGE.

LET'S RENT A SAILBOAT, CATHY.

GREAT. I CAN LIE ON THE DECK AND WRITE POSTCARDS!

HOW ABOUT A GAME OF TENNIS?

GREAT. I CAN WRITE POSTCARDS WHILE WE WAIT FOR A COURT!

HOW ABOUT A ROMANTIC WALK ON THE BEACH?

GREAT. I CAN WRITE POSTCARDS IN THE MOONLIGHT!

HOW MANY?

JUST THE THREE OF US. CATHY, ME, AND THE POSTCARDS.

DISCO

DANCING LIVE BAND

FOR WEEKS I SAVED UP THINGS TO DISCUSS WITH IRVING WHEN WE WERE ON VACATION.

NOW THAT WE'RE ON VACATION I'VE SHOVED THOSE THINGS TO THE BACK AND AM SAVING UP NEW THINGS TO DISCUSS WHEN WE GET HOME. WHEN WE GET HOME I'LL SHOVE THOSE THINGS TO THE BACK AND SAVE UP NEW THINGS.

ONE DAY MY MOUTH WILL OPEN AND ALL THE JUNK I'VE SAVED UP WILL COME POURING OUT FOR EVERYONE TO SEE !!

WANT TO TALK ABOUT SOMETHING, CATHY ?

WHY HAVE A CONVERSATION WHEN YOU CAN HOLD OUT FOR A GARAGE SALE ?

GRIT YOUR TEETH LIKE YOU DID WHEN I HAD TO DUMP MY PURSE OUT IN THE ELEVATOR TO FIND MY ROOM KEY !

"SNAP SNAP"

SCENIC VIEW

PERFECT... NOW GO BERSERK LIKE YOU DID WHEN I SAID, "ANY RESTAURANT IS FINE", AND THEN REJECTED THE ONE YOU PICKED !

"SNAP SNAP SNAP"

GREAT, IRVING... NOW BUG YOUR EYES OUT LIKE YOU DID WHEN I MADE YOU STOP AT A LADIES ROOM FOR THE FIFTEENTH TIME !!

"SNAP!"

SOME PEOPLE BRING HOME SNAPSHOTS. WE BRING HOME LEGENDS.

I SHOULD HAVE THROWN IN THE WHITE SKIRT. NO. THE BLUE SHORTS WOULD HAVE BEEN MORE USEFUL.

...NO. THE RED SUNDRESS. I DEFINITELY SHOULD HAVE BROUGHT THE RED SUNDRESS AND THE TAN SANDALS.

DO YOU BELIEVE THIS, IRVING ?? OUR VACATION IS HALF OVER AND I'M STILL DECIDING WHAT TO PACK !

SO WHAT ? I'M STILL DECIDING WHO TO INVITE.

IN JULY I WATCHED GERALDINE FERRARO AND GOT A WHOLE NEW SENSE FOR MY POTENTIAL IN THE WORLD!

IN AUGUST I WATCHED THE WOMEN AT THE OLYMPICS AND REALIZED THERE ARE NO LIMITS TO WHAT I CAN ACHIEVE IF I TRY !

THIS WOULD HAVE BEEN A GOOD YEAR TO TAKE MY VACATION IN JUNE.

ONE OUNCE OF MACADAMIA NUTS HAS 200 CALORIES, IRVING.

IS THAT A LOT ?

YOU ARE HOLDING THE CALORIC EQUIVALENT OF 13 BLUEBERRY MUFFINS IN YOUR LEFT HAND !

IS THAT A LOT ?

IRVING, YOU HAVE 28,000 CALORIES IN FRONT OF YOU !

IS THAT A LOT ?

NO.

DO YOU **HAVE** TO CALL YOUR MACHINE, AGAIN ?

YES. I'M AFRAID MR. PINKLEY'S FURIOUS WITH ME FOR NOT CALLING IN, MOM'S HYSTERICAL, AND ANDREA'S HURT.

WHAT DID IT SAY ?

MR. PINKLEY'S FURIOUS, MOM'S HYSTERICAL, AND ANDREA'S HURT.

I DON'T KNOW WHY YOU EVEN NEED THAT STUPID MACHINE, CATHY.

I LIKE TO GET MY GUILT CONFIRMED ON TAPE.

31

Panel 1: TWO THREE-HOUR LAYOVERS, AN HOUR AND A HALF WAIT ON THE RUNWAY, AND SIX HOURS IN THE AIR.

Panel 2: SO WHAT IF I LOOK DISGUSTING? WE **ALL** LOOK DISGUSTING! WE'RE ALL TIRED, SWEATY AND DISGUSTING.

Panel 4: THERE'S ALWAYS ONE WOMAN WHO RUINS IT FOR EVERYBODY.

Panel 5: WHERE IS IT?! WHERE IS MY LUGGAGE **THIS** TIME??!!

LOST LUGG

Panel 6: YOUR LUGGAGE HAS TRAVELED 30,000 MILES MORE THAN YOU THIS YEAR, AND QUALIFIED FOR A FREE ROUND-TRIP TICKET TO EUROPE.

Panel 7: ALL THREE PIECES HOPPED A PLANE FOR THE RIVIERA AND ARE HAVING THE TIME OF THEIR LITTLE LIVES!

Panel 8: I HAVEN'T LOST MY LUGGAGE. I'VE BEEN REJECTED BY IT.

LO

Panel 9: IRVING REFUSED TO ASK DIRECTIONS AND WE HAD TO GET TOWED OUT OF THIS JUNGLE AND.... NEVER MIND.

BAGGAGE

Panel 10: THEN CATHY RAN INTO THIS GIFT SHOP AND GOT CONNED INTO PAYING $75 FOR A... ...NEVER MIND.

TO PARKING

Panel 11: THEN THERE WAS THE TIME HE WAS CHANGING CLOTHES AND THE.... NEVER MIND.

PARKING

Panel 12: INDIVIDUALLY, WE HAD FUN. TOGETHER, WE'RE NOT READY TO LAUGH YET.

I'M SICK OF YOU AND I NEVER WANT TO SEE YOU AGAIN !!!

FINE. EXCEPT I'LL HAVE TO COME GET MY 5 ROLLS OF FILM THAT ARE MIXED UP WITH YOURS!

FINE. BUT I'LL HAVE TO PICK UP MY SNEAKERS THAT ARE BURIED IN YOUR LUGGAGE!

FINE. BUT I'LL HAVE TO GET MY TRIP RECEIPTS FROM THE POCKET OF THE JACKET YOU LOST!

FINE. THEN I'LL GET MY VISA CARD, WHICH YOU'LL FIND WHEN YOU EXCAVATE YOUR PURSE !!

WE'RE NOT ORGANIZED ENOUGH TO BREAK UP, SWEETIE.

DRESSING ROOMS

IT'S ME, BUT IT'S A PART OF ME I'M NOT READY TO SHARE WITH THE GENERAL PUBLIC.

THE LOVEBIRD HAS RETURNED FROM VACATION! HOW WAS IT, CATHY?

FINE, CHARLENE.

HOW WERE THE ACCOMMODATIONS ??

FINE. JUST FINE.

AND HOW WAS THE....

FINE! EVERYTHING WAS FINE !!!

SHE CAME BACK WITH A LOT OF COLOR.

ALL SUMMER I TRIED TO HAVE TAN LEGS, AND SEARCHED FOR THE PERFECT PAIR OF WHITE PANTS.

NOW WE'RE MOVING INTO FALL.

NOW I WILL HAVE WHITE LEGS AND SEARCH FOR THE PERFECT PAIR OF TAN PANTS.

I LOVE THE VARIETY OF THE SEASONS.

YEECH! COVER UP THE BANK ADS SO I DON'T HAVE TO SEE THE INTEREST I'D BE EARNING IF I'D TAKEN 5 SECONDS TO CHANGE MY ACCOUNT!!

YAACK! TURN THE PAGE SO I DON'T GET REMINDED HOW IGNORANT I AM ON FOREIGN AFFAIRS!!

BLEAH! COVER THE STORIES ON WOMEN MY AGE WHO ARE EARNING $100,000 A YEAR! WAD UP ALL ADS ON HEALTH CLUBS!!

WHY DON'T YOU JUST WATCH THE NEWS ON TV, CATHY?

I LIKE THE PERSONAL INVOLVEMENT I GET WITH MY NEWSPAPER.

I'M NOT QUITE READY TO HEAR THE VERSION OF YOUR VACATION YOU'D TELL YOUR GIRLFRIENDS, CATHY, BUT I'M DEFINITELY BEYOND THE "GRANDMOTHER VERSION."

I WANT A VERSION THAT ACKNOWLEDGES MY GROWTH AS AN '80s MOTHER, AND MY OPEN, ACCEPTING MIND TOWARD MODERN DATING!

HOW ABOUT YOUR USUAL VERSION, MOM?

THANK YOU, SWEETIE.

WHY ARE YOU CUTTING THE SIZE TAG OUT OF YOUR NEW SKIRT?

I DON'T WANT ANYONE TO SEE WHAT SIZE IT IS, ANDREA.

WHY WOULD ANYONE BE LOOKING AT THE SIZE TAG ON THE INSIDE OF YOUR SKIRT?

YOU NEVER KNOW. IT MIGHT BE LYING AROUND AND SOMEONE WOULD PICK IT UP AND LOOK AT IT.

WHAT KIND OF PERSON WOULD PICK UP A PIECE OF CLOTHING IN SOMEONE ELSE'S HOME AND LOOK AT THE SIZE TAG?? YOU'RE OUT OF YOUR MIND, CATHY!!!

SPOKEN LIKE A REAL SIZE 7.

WE'RE GOING TO BE LATE FOR WORK, CATHY.

IRVING'S PICKING ME UP RIGHT FROM THE OFFICE TODAY. I WANT TO PUT ON MY ONE PERFECT OUTFIT.

LET'S RACE OUT TO THE MALL FOR LUNCH.

NO, THANKS. IRVING'S PICKING ME UP RIGHT FROM THE OFFICE. I DON'T WANT TO MESS UP MY ONE PERFECT OUTFIT.

WHY DON'T YOU PUT ON YOUR JACKET IF YOU'RE COLD?

IRVING'S PICKING ME UP RIGHT FROM THE OFFICE. I DON'T WANT TO WRINKLE MY ONE PERFECT OUTFIT.

HI, HONEY. WANT TO STOP BY YOUR PLACE AND CHANGE BEFORE DINNER?

WHY HAVEN'T YOU HEARD FROM IRVING, CATHY?

I DON'T KNOW.

I SNEAKED PAST HIS APARTMENT AND TRIED TO PEEK IN THE WINDOW... I HID IN THE BUSHES NEAR HIS OFFICE SO I COULD SEE IF HE WAS LEAVING WITH ANYONE...

I PAID A FRIEND TO SPY ON HIM AT HIS RACQUETBALL CLUB.... AND I CALLED HIS PLACE AT 2:00am AND THEN HUNG UP WHEN HE ANSWERED. STILL NO CLUES.

WHY DON'T YOU JUST CALL AND ASK HIM WHAT'S GOING ON?

I HAVE MY PRIDE, ANDREA.

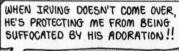

SCOOPED NECK ANGORA SWEATER: CATHY HAD A HOT DATE.

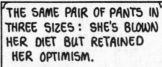
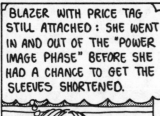

BLAZER WITH PRICE TAG STILL ATTACHED: SHE WENT IN AND OUT OF THE "POWER IMAGE PHASE" BEFORE SHE HAD A CHANCE TO GET THE SLEEVES SHORTENED.

THE SAME PAIR OF PANTS IN THREE SIZES: SHE'S BLOWN HER DIET BUT RETAINED HER OPTIMISM.

WHAT ARE YOU DOING, MOM?

I COULDN'T FIND YOUR DIARY SO I'M READING YOUR CLOSET.

MR. PINKLEY WANTS THIS IN AN HOUR. SHOULD I DO IT, OR SHOULD I TELL HIM HIS DEADLINE IS TOTALLY UNREASONABLE?

AM I RISING TO A CHALLENGE OR CATERING TO HIS WHIMS?

AM I ESCALATING MY CAREER, OR AM I LOCKING MYSELF IN THIS POSITION BECAUSE I'M THE ONLY ONE WHO WOULD PUT UP WITH HIS LUDICROUS DEMANDS?!!

HOW'S IT COMING, CATHY?

I'M STILL ANALYZING THE PROJECT.

$98 FOR THIS OLD RAG? ARE THEY OUT OF THEIR MINDS?!

THAT'S THE LOOK, MOTHER.

IT'S A CLEANING RAG!

IT'S VERY CHIC.

IT'S AN OUTRAGE!!

I LIKE IT!!

YOU LIKE IT??

I LOVE IT AND I JUST MIGHT BUY IT!!!

DID YOU WANT THAT?

$98 FOR THIS OLD RAG? ARE YOU OUT OF YOUR MIND?!

 BLEAH! WHAT A HIDEOUS DAY! I CAN'T WAIT TO GET TO AEROBICS CLASS AND WORK OFF THIS TENSION!

 I'M GOING TO GO LIFT WEIGHTS AND SWIM SOME LAPS.

 I'M GOING TO DO A 10K RUN AND GO THROUGH SOME ISOMETRICS IN THE JACUZZI.

 DOESN'T ANYBODY EAT PIE ANYMORE?

 HI, IRVING. THINGS HAVE GONE CRAZY AT WORK. I'M GOING TO HAVE TO SKIP TONIGHT.

OH. I WAS GOING TO CALL AND SAY I WAS TOO BUSY AND HAD TO SKIP TONIGHT.

 I WAS GOING TO CALL EARLIER AND TELL YOU, BUT I WAS TOO BUSY.

I KNEW AT 7:30 THIS MORNING THAT I WAS TOO BUSY.

 GOOD THING YOU DIDN'T CALL BECAUSE I WOULD HAVE BEEN TOO BUSY TO ANSWER!

I'M TOO BUSY TO DISCUSS IT!!

 COMPETITIVE DATE CANCELING.

 SEE WHAT YOU CAN DO WITH THE FALLON PROJECT, CATHY.

 RUSTLE RUSTLE STAPLE CLIP RUSTLE

 MY RIGHT BRAIN TOOK OVER.

WOMEN WOULD LIKE TO TAKE THE INITIATIVE IN RELATION-SHIPS MORE, IRVING, BUT WE'RE AFRAID MEN WILL INTERPRET IT AS "LOOSE."

SOMETIMES WE'D LIKE TO GET MORE LOOSE, BUT WE'RE AFRAID MEN WILL INTER-PRET IT AS "INSINCERE."

SOMETIMES WE'D EVEN LIKE TO GET MORE INSINCERE, BUT WE'RE AFRAID MEN WILL INTERPRET IT AS, UM, "IN-SINCERE". THEREFORE, I FEEL I'VE MORE THAN DONE MY PART. GOODNIGHT!

EVERY TIME WE HAVE A DISCUSSION, I KNOW LESS ABOUT WHAT'S GOING ON.

ON MONDAY I RESTARTED MY DIET.

ON TUESDAY I RESTARTED MY DIET AND RESTARTED MY EXERCISE PROGRAM.

ON WEDNESDAY I RESTARTED MY DIET, MY EXERCISE PRO-GRAM, AND MY OFFICE OR-GANIZATION PLAN.... ON THURSDAY I RESTARTED MY DIET, MY EXERCISE PRO-GRAM, MY OFFICE PLAN, AND MY ALL-NEW BUDGET.

WITH EVERY DAY I HAVE MORE TO BE OPTIMISTIC ABOUT.

CATHY NEEDS ME. I CAN FEEL IT.

SHE'S UNHAPPY ABOUT SOMETHING AT WORK. I CAN SENSE IT.

HER GIRLFRIEND'S ANNOYED... HER BOYFRIEND DIDN'T SHOW UP...HER PHONE PAYMENT BOUNCED... HER CAR NEEDS OIL AND HER BROCCOLI JUST WENT BAD!

MY WIFE: THE CABLE TV OF MOTHERLY INTUITION.

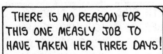

I COOKED 18,000 MEALS FOR YOU WHEN YOU WERE GROWING UP, CATHY. YOU DIDN'T APPRECIATE IT.

I DROVE YOU TO 400 PIANO LESSONS. YOU DIDN'T APPRECIATE IT. I DRAGGED YOU TO CULTURAL EVENTS. YOU DIDN'T APPRECIATE IT.

TODAY I RETURNED A SLIP YOU BOUGHT LAST YEAR THAT YOU WERE TOO EMBARRASSED TO TAKE BACK... AND NOW YOU'RE TREATING ME LIKE THE QUEEN OF ENGLAND.

I COULD HAVE SAVED MYSELF A LOT OF GRIEF IF I'D JUST GIVEN BIRTH AND DROPPED YOU OFF AT THE MALL.

LET'S PIG OUT ON DONUTS AND COFFEE LIKE THE GOOD OLD DAYS, BETH!

I COULDN'T. CAFFEINE AND SUGAR AREN'T GOOD FOR MY BABY.

LET'S SIT HERE AND COMPLAIN ABOUT THE MEN IN OUR LIVES!!

BOB AND I HAVE NEVER BEEN CLOSER.

LET'S COMPARE CAREER MOVES AND PICK APART OUR RELATIONSHIPS WITH OUR MOTHERS!!

MY CAREER IS ON HOLD. MOM AND I ARE ON A SPIRITUAL NEW WAVELENGTH.

ONE BABY, 500 MIRACLES.

IF YOU THINK I'VE BEEN TRYING TO TRICK YOU INTO A COMMITMENT, YOU'VE MISUNDERSTOOD ME, IRVING.

WE BOTH HAVE A LOT OF DEMANDS ON OUR TIME, AND THE LAST THING EITHER OF US NEEDS IS TO FEEL OBLIGATED OR PUSHED.

I RESPECT YOU FAR TOO MUCH TO EVER RESORT TO SOME KIND OF CHEAP, EMOTIONAL AMBUSH.

"HOW TO WIN A MAN": COSMOPOLITAN MAGAZINE; 1984; PAGES 91-93!!

cathy by Cathy Guisewite

NO.
NO, I'M BUSY.
NO, I HAVE PLANS.
NO, I'M BOOKED.
NO THANK YOU.
NOPE.
NOT TODAY.
NOT TOMORROW.
NOT EVER.
NO WAY.
HUH, UH, HONEY.

RING RING!

HI, CATHY. WANT TO GO OUT?

SURE!

WHEN RANDY CALLS AGAIN, I'LL SAY, "SORRY, RANDY. I'M JUST NOT INTERESTED".... IT'S BETTER TO GET THE NEWS OVER THE PHONE.

RING RING!

WHEN RANDY ARRIVES, I'LL SAY, "SORRY, RANDY, WE'RE THROUGH".. ... IT'S BETTER TO GET THE NEWS IN PERSON.

WHEN WE'RE HAVING DINNER, I'LL SAY, "RANDY, THIS IS IT!"... IT'S BETTER TO GET THE NEWS IN A PUBLIC PLACE.

WHEN DESSERT IS SERVED, I'LL SAY, "RANDY, IT'S OVER BETWEEN US!"... IT'S BETTER TO GET THE NEWS AFTER A NICE MEAL.

WHEN RANDY DROPS ME OFF, I'LL SAY, "RANDY, GOODBYE FOREVER!".. ... IT'S BETTER TO GET THE NEWS WHEN YOU DON'T HAVE A BIG CAR RIDE AHEAD OF YOU.

WHEN WE'VE HAD ONE CUP OF COFFEE, I'LL SAY, "RANDY, IT'S FINITO!!"... ... IT'S BETTER TO GET THE NEWS WHEN YOU'RE NOT STANDING IN THE HALL.

...WELL, I'D BETTER BE GOING, CATHY. THANKS. I HAD A WONDERFUL TIME!!

THANK YOU, RANDY. ME TOO!

WHEN RANDY CALLS AGAIN, I'LL SAY, "SORRY, RANDY. I'M JUST NOT INTERESTED".....

DON'T LEAVE ME, RUTHANN! YOU'RE THE ONLY WOMAN WHO EVER FIXED MY COFFEE RIGHT!

I HAVE TO GO GIVE BIRTH.

I DON'T KNOW WHERE ANYTHING IS! I DON'T KNOW HOW THE PHONES WORK!!

GIVE IT UP, MR. PINKLEY.

SHE KNOWS ALL MY SECRETS!! SHE KNOWS HOW I LIKE MY MEMOS TYPED!

SHE'LL COME BACK AS SOON AS WE HAVE A DAY-CARE PLAN.

DON'T BE RIDICULOUS. THE OFFICE IS NO PLACE FOR BABIES.

ATTENTION ALL EMPLOYEES: TOMORROW IS MY 30TH BIRTHDAY.

I HAVE BEEN BUILDING UP TO A MAJOR EMOTIONAL CRISIS FOR 29 YEARS AND 364 DAYS, AND I WILL NOT BE ROBBED OF IT BY ANY OF YOU 22-YEAR-OLDS DECIDING TO GIVE BIRTH ON MY BIG DAY.

IF YOU MOMMIES-TO-BE HAVE ONE SHRED OF COMPASSION, YOU WILL HOLD OUT UNTIL THE.....

JUST MY LUCK. THE ONE DAY ANYONE LISTENS TO MY ANNOUNCEMENTS, I INDUCE LABOR.

HOW'S IT GOING, CHARLENE?

RUTHANN HAD A SIX-POUNDER, MARGO'S DILATTING, JAN'S DELIVERING...

FIVE JERKS I ONCE THREW OUT OF MY LIFE HAVE TRANSFORMED THEMSELVES INTO NURTURING FATHERS... PRINCESS DI JUST HATCHED HER SECOND HEIR TO THE THRONE...

TODAY IS MY 30TH BIRTHDAY, AND THE CLOSEST I'LL GET TO MOTHERHOOD IS PICKING UP AFTER MY INFANTILE BOYFRIEND, FRANKIE!!

GET ME A CUP OF COFFEE, WILL YA, CHARLENE?

I LOVE THE FESTIVE ATMOSPHERE OF BIRTHDAY WEEK AT THE OFFICE.

"30: THE DESPERATE YEARS," BY CHARLENE McGUIRE.

..."AGE SNEAKED UP ON ME LIKE AN 'OIL OF OLAY' AD," BY CHARLENE McGUIRE.

CHARLENE, 30 ISN'T OLD ANY-MORE! YOU'RE A YOUNG, VI-TAL WOMAN WITH THE WHOLE WORLD AT YOUR FINGER-TIPS! LOOK AT YOURSELF!!

"I MARRIED A ROLODEX," BY CHARLENE McGUIRE.

"EMBARK ON YOUR CAREER," THEY SAID. I EMBARKED.

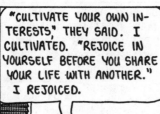

"CULTIVATE YOUR OWN IN-TERESTS," THEY SAID. I CULTIVATED. "REJOICE IN YOURSELF BEFORE YOU SHARE YOUR LIFE WITH ANOTHER." I REJOICED.

WHILE I'VE BEEN EMBARK-ING, CULTIVATING AND RE-JOICING, EVERYONE ELSE SNEAKED OFF WITH ALL THE MEN!!!

ANYTHING I CAN DO FOR YOU?

RUN FOR YOUR LIFE.

ATTENTION ALL EMPLOYEES: THE OFFICE BABIES HAVE ALL BEEN BORN, AND I'M ABOUT TO ANNOUNCE THE WINNERS OF THE "PREGNANCY POOL."

LOOK AT THIS CORPORATE SPIRIT AND ENERGY, CATHY! AND FOR WHAT? A TOTAL POT OF $5.00!

WHY CAN'T WE DIRECT SOME OF THAT SAME PASSION TOWARD AN ACTUAL CLIENT?!

WE COULDN'T WIN AS MUCH.

SIX WOMEN ARE OUT HAVING BABIES, CATHY, AND WHAT DOES THAT LEAVE ?? THE MEN! THE BACKBONE OF THE CORPORATION !

THE MEN MADE THE CORPORATION, AND THE MEN WILL CARRY ON !! SEND IN MY MEN, CATHY !!

YOU GRANTED THEM ALL PATERNITY LEAVE DURING A DRUNKEN STUPOR AT THE COMPANY PICNIC LAST SUMMER, MR. PINKLEY.

WHAT'S WRONG WITH HIM?

HE'S HAVING AN EMOTIONAL RESPONSE TO FATHERING.

AREN'T YOU NERVOUS TAKING IT OUT OF THE HOUSE ?

WHEN WE FIRST BROUGHT HIM HOME I WAS AFRAID TO EVEN TOUCH HIM.

WE READ 50 DIFFERENT BOOKS AND TALKED TO 50 FRIENDS, AND GOT 100 DIFFERENT OPINIONS. I REALLY WONDERED IF WE'D MADE THE RIGHT DECISION.

OH, SURE, WE'VE ALREADY MADE MISTAKES...BUT ONE LITTLE RESPONSE FROM HIM AND EVERY SLEEPLESS NIGHT IS WORTHWHILE !

A BABY ! LET ME SEE !!

KNOCK KNOCK !

THOSE OF US WHO AREN'T HAVING BABIES ARE HAVING COMPUTERS.

I THOUGHT YOU WANTED KIDS, TOO, CATHY.

I'M STILL TRYING TO FIGURE OUT MY CAREER, CHARLENE.

THE SINGLE, CHILDLESS CAREER WOMAN IS PASSÉ. A PHASE-OUT !

I'M NOT EVEN SURE IF I'M IN THE RIGHT FIELD YET.

CATHY, THE ENTIRE WORLD IS BECOMING A PARENT. DOESN'T THAT BOTHER YOU ??

I GUESS I'M USED TO IT.

EVERYONE ALWAYS SWITCHES TO A NEW IMAGE BEFORE I GET THE ALTERATIONS DONE ON THE OLD ONE.

WHO'S GOING TO START?

YOU START.

NO. YOU START.

"CATHY, WE HATE TO PRY, BUT..."

NO. WE LIKE TO PRY.

YES. WE LIKE TO PRY.

WE LOVE TO PRY.

WE LIVE TO PRY!

WE'RE PROUD OF HOW WE PRY!

OUR PRYING IS STATE OF THE ART!

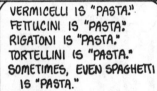

HI, CATHY. WHAT'S NEW?

NOTHING.

I WORK BETTER ALONE.

WANT SOME PASTA SALAD, CATHY?

THAT ISN'T "PASTA". THAT'S MACARONI, IRVING.

VERMICELLI IS "PASTA." FETTUCINI IS "PASTA." RIGATONI IS "PASTA." TORTELLINI IS "PASTA." SOMETIMES, EVEN SPAGHETTI IS "PASTA."

BUT TODAY, AND FOR THE ENTIRE FORSEEABLE FUTURE, MACARONI IS STILL "FAT"!!

SALAD BAR

I'D HATE FOR SUCH A CLOSE FRIEND TO GET TO LOSE ITS IMAGE THAT EASILY.

SOMETIMES MEN WONDER IF WE REALLY NEED THEM.... TONIGHT I REALLY NEED IRVING, BUT TONIGHT I LOOK TERRIBLE.

IS IT BETTER TO SEE HIM WHEN I LOOK TERRIBLE AND REALLY NEED HIM... OR IS IT BETTER TO WAIT UNTIL I LOOK GREAT AND THEN TRY TO RE-CREATE HOW MUCH I NEEDED HIM?

MEN ARE GOING TO CONTINUE TO WONDER IF WE REALLY NEED THEM.

FOAMING ORCHID BATH OIL...

HERBAL FRAGRANCE SHAMPOO... FLORAL BATH BEADS... HONEYSUCKLE BODY SCRUB...

WILD FLOWER SKIN SPRAY... LOTUS BLOSSOM BODY LOTION... MUSKY BATH POWDER...

LAVENDER MIST DEODORANT... APRICOT MOISTURIZER...

ESSENCE OF ROSE COLOGNE... STRAWBERRY HAND CREME...

WINTERGREEN BREATH SPRAY...

UNLEADED GASOLINE.

WHEN I STARTED MY JOB, IT WAS SUCH A CHALLENGE. I REALLY WANTED TO CARE.

I CARED SO MUCH THAT I GOT DEPENDED ON... SO NOW I HAVE TO CARE. IRVING, I DON'T WANT TO CARE IF I'M OBLIGATED TO CARE!

YES! THAT'S US, CATHY! THAT'S WHAT I'VE BEEN TRYING TO SAY IS THE PROBLEM WITH US!!

I CAN'T BELIEVE IT. MY CAREER IS PARALLELING MY BOYFRIEND'S LOVE LIFE.

THIS DINNER LOOKS GOOD, CATHY.

IT'S GREAT! I GET IT ALL THE TIME!

I STARTED GETTING THAT ONE MONTHS AGO!

I'VE EATEN THAT PARTICULAR DINNER SO MANY TIMES I CAN'T EVEN STAND TO LOOK AT THE PACKAGE ANYMORE!!

ONE-UPSMANSHIP STRIKES THE FROZEN FOOD DEPARTMENT.

DON'T WASH THAT, MOM. I'LL JUST RUN IT THROUGH AGAIN.

ISN'T THIS THE SAME FORK YOU MADE ME PUT BACK IN THE DISHWASHER 3 MONTHS AGO?

MAYBE.

CATHY, THE SAME DIRT ON THIS SAME FORK HAS BEEN THROUGH THE DISHWASHER 20 TIMES.

THE DIRT IS SOLDERED ONTO THAT FORK BY NOW. THE DIRT IS ON THE BRINK OF BECOMING A PERMANENT PART OF THAT FORK'S PERSONALITY!!

CAN I HELP IT IF I BELIEVE IN SECOND CHANCES?

IN HIGH SCHOOL, WHEN I HAD ALL THE TIME IN THE WORLD, EVERY GUY I SAW LOOKED PERFECT TO ME.

...IN COLLEGE, WHEN MY WHOLE LIFE STRETCHED BEFORE ME, EVERY GUY I SAW LOOKED PERFECT TO ME.

...TODAY, WHEN MY LOOKS, MY SHAPE AND MY CLOCK ARE GOING AT FULL SPEED, ONE GUY IN FIVE HUNDRED LOOKS VAGUELY ACCEPTABLE.

NOW THAT I FINALLY HAVE A CRITICAL EYE, IT NEEDS A BIFOCAL.

WHY WON'T YOU SUGGEST A FRIEND TO FIX CHARLENE UP WITH, IRVING?

BECAUSE YOU'LL WIND UP HATING ME, CATHY.

YOU'LL HATE ME. CHARLENE WILL HATE ME. CHARLENE WILL HATE YOU. CHARLENE AND MY FRIEND WILL HATE EACH OTHER.

MY FRIEND'S FRIENDS WILL HATE YOU. YOUR FRIENDS WILL HATE MY FRIENDS. CHARLENE'S MOTHER WILL HATE YOUR MOTHER, AND I'LL HATE MYSELF FOR GETTING TALKED INTO IT!!

HOW MANY CHANCES DO WE GET TO INVOLVE SO MANY PEOPLE WE KNOW IN ONE ACTIVITY?

OH, GET REAL! WHO HAS A RELATIONSHIP LIKE THAT?! HAH! LISTEN TO HER!!

SHE EXPECTS HIM TO BELIEVE THAT?? HAH! DRIVEL! DRIVEL!!

I SEE YOU'RE ENGAGING IN AMERICA'S FAVORITE PASTIME.

YEAH...

SCOFFING ON THE OUTSIDE, TAKING NOTES ON THE INSIDE.

MARKETING? REALLY? I HAVE SOME FRIENDS IN MARKETING I CAN INTRODUCE YOU TO.

AND I HAVE SOME FRIENDS IN SALES I CAN INTRODUCE YOU TO.

THEN MAYBE YOU CAN MEET MY MEDIA FRIENDS. OH, AND YOU'LL LOVE MY RAC-QUETBALL FRIENDS.

YOU'LL HAVE TO MEET MY LAWYER FRIENDS.

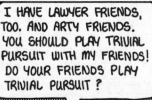

I HAVE LAWYER FRIENDS, TOO. AND ARTY FRIENDS. YOU SHOULD PLAY TRIVIAL PURSUIT WITH MY FRIENDS! DO YOUR FRIENDS PLAY TRIVIAL PURSUIT?

WASN'T DATING HARD ENOUGH WHEN ONLY TWO OF US WERE SUPPOSED TO GET ALONG?

I WONDER IF IRVING FOUND OUT I HAD DRINKS WITH THAT GUY YESTER-DAY.

I WONDER IF CATHY KNOWS I SAW BRENDA THIS WEEK.

I WONDER IF HE SUSPECTS I'VE ALREADY BEEN TO THIS NEW RESTAU-RANT WITH SOMEONE ELSE.

I WONDER IF SHE CAN TELL I'VE BEEN THINK-ING ABOUT KAREN ALL NIGHT.

I'LL TAKE IT! I'LL TAKE THE CHECK!!

IT'S THE NEW SYSTEM. WHOEVER FEELS THE GUILTIEST PAYS.

COME ON, CATHY. I'LL WALK OUT WITH YOU.

UM... OKAY, MOM. I JUST WANT TO MAKE SURE I HAVE EVERYTHING.

HOW MUCH COULD YOU NEED? YOU'RE ONLY MEETING IRVING FOR DINNER.

YEAH... WELL, UM... I'LL JUST MAKE SURE....

MY GENERATION NEVER WASTED THIS MUCH TIME GETTING READY FOR ONE LITTLE EVENING!

YOUR GENERATION NEVER HAD TO PACK FOR YOUR DATES.

IRVING, PLEASE DON'T LEAVE YOUR CUP ON THE ARM OF MY COUCH.

CATHY, I'VE SEEN YOU LEAVE CLOTHES HEAPED IN THE KITCHEN, DISHES PILED IN THE BATHROOM, BILLS STUFFED IN THE STEREO CABINET AND SHOES THROWN EVERYWHERE.

WHY WOULD YOU CARE IF I LEAVE ONE LITTLE CUP ON THE ARM OF YOUR COUCH??

IT ISN'T THE WAY I LIKE MY MESSES TO LOOK!!!

WHAT DO YOU MEAN, YOU CAN'T HAVE LUNCH WITH ME, CATHY?! WE PLANNED THIS A WEEK AGO!

DON'T LISTEN TO HIM! I HAVE THE INSIDE STORY ON THE MARTIN ACCOUNT!

YOUR PAYMENT IS OVERDUE. ALL SERVICE WILL BE DISCONNECTED IF NOT PAID IMMEDIATELY!

IT'S GETTING HARDER AND HARDER TO LIVE WITHOUT STEREO.

HOW ARE THINGS WITH IRVING, CATHY?

OKAY, CHARLENE. ...NORMAL.

WE'RE NOT GOING UP. WE'RE NOT GOING DOWN. WE'RE JUST, YOU KNOW...NORMAL.

AND I CAN'T STAND IT! I WANT TO GO ONE WAY OR THE OTHER BUT I CAN'T STAND BEING IN THE NORMAL MIDDLE!!

...THIS WOMAN ACTUALLY WONDERS WHY HER MAINTENANCE DIETS NEVER WORK.

56

Panel 1: THE NEKERVISES GATHER AROUND THE THANKSGIVING TABLE AND WRITE ALL THEIR CHRISTMAS NOTES.

BLEAH!

Panel 2: THE JOHNSTONS SPEND THANKSGIVING CREATING HOMEMADE GIFT WRAP FOR THE HOMEMADE GIFTS THEY WORKED ALL SUMMER ON.

BLEAH!

Panel 3: WE SPEND THE ENTIRE WEEKEND EATING.

YEAH! MORE PIE! MORE PIE!!

Panel 4: THERE'S NOTHING LIKE THE HOLIDAYS TO DEFINE WHAT'S IMPORTANT TO YOUR FAMILY.

Panel 5: HOLIDAY OR NOT, I BROUGHT WORK HOME AND I HAVE TO WORK, MOM!

OH! YOU HAVE TO WORK! SHE HAS TO WORK, DEAR!

Panel 6: I CLEANED OFF THE COFFEE TABLE SO YOU CAN WORK.

YOU SHOULD WORK FOR TWO HOURS, CATHY.

WHY NOT WORK FOR THREE HOURS?

Panel 7: SHOULDN'T YOU START WORKING?

SHE ISN'T WORKING?

WE GOT YOU ALL SET UP TO WORK.

GO AHEAD, WORK!

Panel 8: IN TWO MINUTES I'VE GONE FROM REVELING IN MY CAREER TO NOT PRACTICING THE PIANO.

Panel 9: CATHY, YOU FOUGHT WITH YOURSELF FOR SIX HOURS ABOUT WHETHER OR NOT TO TOUCH THE LEFTOVER SWEET POTATOES...

Panel 10: YOU FOUGHT WITH YOURSELF FOR TWO HOURS ABOUT NOT HAVING ANOTHER PIECE OF PIE... AND NOW YOU'RE EATING EVERYTHING IN YOUR PATH WITHOUT A SECOND'S THOUGHT!!

Panel 11: I CAN'T BELIEVE YOU'VE LET YOURSELF BE TOTALLY DEFEATED!!

I'M NOT DEFEATED, ANDREA.

Panel 12: I'VE STREAMLINED MY RATIONALIZATION PROCESS.

START, YOU MISERABLE PILE OF GARBAGE!!

START, YOU DISGUSTING, NON-PAID-FOR JUNK HEAP!!!

START, YOU PATHETIC INSULT TO THE AUTOMOTIVE INDUSTRY!!!

I WON'T BE IN TODAY, MR. PINKLEY. I'VE DEVELOPED A SORE THROAT.

I DON'T HAVE TIME TO DO THIS PROJECT RIGHT, CHARLENE.

I DON'T HAVE TIME TO DO ANYTHING RIGHT, CATHY.

I DON'T HAVE TIME TO SEE IRVING.

I DON'T HAVE TIME FOR FRANKIE.

I DON'T HAVE TIME TO WORK OUT.

I DON'T HAVE TIME TO CLEAN.

I DON'T HAVE TIME TO THINK.

I DON'T HAVE TIME TO SLEEP.

WE ALWAYS HAVE TIME FOR WHAT'S REALLY IMPORTANT.

COMPLAINING.

TWO YEARS AGO YOU SAID, "THIS DRESS WILL FIT ALL YOUR PARTY NEEDS FOR YEARS TO COME." ONE DAY AFTER THE HOLIDAYS, IT LOOKED RIDICULOUS.

LAST YEAR YOU SAID, "THIS DRESS WILL FIT ALL YOUR PARTY NEEDS FOR YEARS TO COME." ONE DAY AFTER THE HOLIDAYS, IT LOOKED RIDICULOUS.

WHAT COULD YOU POSSIBLY SAY THAT WOULD MAKE ME SPEND $200 FOR YET ANOTHER HOLIDAY DRESS?!

IT WILL FIT ALL YOUR PARTY NEEDS FOR YEARS TO COME.

SOLD!

NOTHING QUITE MATCHES THE THRILL OF HAVING AN ONGOING RELATIONSHIP WITH A CUSTOMER.

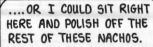

I COULD GO OVER TO THAT MAN, INTRODUCE MYSELF, INVITE HIM TO LEAVE THIS BORING PARTY WITH ME, AND CHANGE THE ENTIRE COURSE OF BOTH OUR LIVES....

.....OR I COULD SIT RIGHT HERE AND POLISH OFF THE REST OF THESE NACHOS.

SHOULD IT BOTHER ME THAT I FIND BOTH IDEAS EQUALLY APPEALING?

I'M GOING TO GO TALK TO THAT GUY, CHARLENE!

IF YOU FEEL YOU HAVE TO STOOP TO THAT LEVEL, FINE.

I THOUGHT YOU'D DEVELOPED A LITTLE MORE DIGNITY THAN THAT, CATHY. I THOUGHT YOU WERE **ABOVE** FLINGING YOURSELF AT SOME HUNK IN A 3-PIECE SUIT!!

OH.

HI YA, CUTIE! I'M CHARLENE!

THERE'S A FINE LINE BETWEEN SISTERHOOD AND SIBLING RIVALRY.

HOW WAS I SUPPOSED TO KNOW HE WAS MARRIED?

I WASN'T.

IN SPITE OF ALL WE'VE GONE THROUGH, A MARRIED **WOMAN** WHO DOESN'T WEAR A RING IS STILL A "WEIRDO," BUT A MARRIED **MAN** WHO DOESN'T WEAR A RING IS "HEY, JUST A GUY WHO DOESN'T LIKE RINGS"!

HAH!

UNTIL MEN START IDENTIFYING THEIR MARITAL STATUS, THEY DON'T DESERVE TO BE APPROACHED!!!

CHARLENE McGUIRE: A UNITED FRONT OF ONE.

Panel 1: HE'S A **DOCTOR**?? CATHY, YOU ASKED HIM OUT AND HE'S A **DOCTOR**!!?!

Panel 2: CHARLENE, GET A GRIP ON YOURSELF. BRIGHT, SUCCESSFUL WOMEN DO NOT LEAP UP AND DOWN IN THE LADIES ROOM SCREAMING, "HE'S A DOCTOR!" ANYMORE.

Panel 4: HE'S NOT A LAWYER!!!

Panel 5: AT WHAT POINT WHEN YOU MEET SOMEONE NEW ARE YOU SUPPOSED TO MENTION YOU'RE ALREADY DATING SOMEONE ELSE, CHARLENE?

Panel 6: TO BRING IT UP THE SECOND YOU MEET SOMEONE MIGHT SEEM PREMATURE.... TO BRING IT UP AFTER EVEN FIVE MINUTES MIGHT SEEM TOO LATE....

Panel 7: TO NOT MENTION IT AT ALL IS AN ABSOLUTE, GUARANTEED SET-UP FOR A HIDEOUS CONFRONTATION DOWN THE LINE!!

Panel 8: YOU DIDN'T TELL MAX ABOUT IRVING, DID YOU, CATHY? / I DECIDED TO GO WITH THE SURE THING.

Panel 9: ATTENTION ALL EMPLOYEES: IN LIEU OF A HOLIDAY PARTY THIS YEAR, I HAVE SUGGESTED THAT MR. PINKLEY PAY FOR ALL OF US TO ACCOMPANY CATHY ON HER FIRST DATE WITH DR. MAX.

Panel 10: EVERYONE INTERESTED IN WATCHING OUR FAVORITE CORPORATE DYNAMO REVERT TO THE EMOTIONAL STATE OF A 14-YEAR-OLD, PLEASE SIGN....

Panel 11: SMASH BOINK BAM

Panel 12: THE LENGTHS I'LL GO TO TO GET SOMEONE ELSE TO PUT UP THE CHRISTMAS DECORATIONS.

"DEAR FRIENDS, MERRY CHRISTMAS! OUR CATHY IS DOING BRILLIANTLY AT WORK AND HAS BEGUN DATING A HANDSOME **DOCTOR**!"

"HE'S..."

WHAT KIND OF DOCTOR IS HE, CATHY?

GYNECOLOGIST.

"DEAR FRIENDS, NOTHING NEW IN THIS HAPPY HOUSEHOLD...."

WHY IS IT THAT EVERYWHERE I LOOK THERE'S A PERFECT GIFT FOR THE MAN I'M TRYING TO BREAK UP WITH, AND NOTHING FOR THE MAN I'M TRYING TO DATE??

VERY SIMPLE. IT'S COMPANY POLICY TO HIDE ALL APPROPRIATE GIFTS, AND DISPLAY ONLY THOSE ITEMS THAT WOULD WREAK HAVOC ON YOUR LIFE IF YOU BOUGHT THEM.

IT'S OUR LITTLE WAY OF SAYING, "WHERE WERE YOU LAST JULY WHEN WE WERE DESPERATE FOR YOUR BUSINESS?"!

WHAT WE LOSE IN SATISFIED CUSTOMERS, WE GAIN IN SATISFIED SALESCLERKS.

"HIM"

YOU WENT SHOPPING FOR GIFTS AND YOU ACTUALLY CAME HOME WITH GIFTS??

OF COURSE I CAME HOME WITH GIFTS.

USUALLY YOU GO SHOPPING FOR GIFTS AND COME HOME WITH FIVE BAGS OF CLOTHES FOR YOURSELF.

ANDREA, AN INTELLIGENT WOMAN IN THESE TIGHT ECONOMIC TIMES DOES NOT WALTZ IN AT CHRISTMASTIME WITH FIVE BAGS OF CLOTHES FOR HERSELF!!

SORRY, CATHY.

...WHEN IT'S SO EASY TO HIDE THEM IN THE TRUNK OF HER CAR.

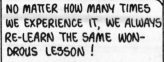

Panel 1: I LOVE CHRISTMAS EVE, CATHY. / YEAH, ME TOO, MOM.

Panel 2: NO MATTER HOW MANY TIMES WE EXPERIENCE IT, WE ALWAYS RE-LEARN THE SAME WONDROUS LESSON!

Panel 4: WRAP GIFTS FIRST, CLEAN HOUSE SECOND.

Panel 5: DON'T CHOP OFF OUR HEADS, MOM. / I'M NOT THE ONE WHO CHOPS OFF HEADS. YOUR FATHER DOES THAT!

Panel 6: HA, HA! YOUR MOTHER DOES THE OUT-OF-FOCUS WORK! / HA, HA, AND CATHY WAITS UNTIL EVERYONE'S EYES ARE SHUT... HA, HA ...OKAY, HOLD IT... READY...AND...

CLICK! ...WHIRRR...

Panel 7: OUT OF FOCUS, HEADS CHOPPED OFF, AND EYES SHUT.

Panel 8: SOMETIMES IT TAKES A MOTHER TO BRING A FAMILY TOGETHER AT CHRISTMAS.

Panel 9: I DIDN'T SPEND ENOUGH... I DIDN'T SPEND ENOUGH... / I SPENT TOO MUCH... I SPENT TOO MUCH...

Panel 11: I SPENT TOO MUCH... I SPENT TOO MUCH... / I DIDN'T SPEND ENOUGH... I DIDN'T SPEND ENOUGH...

Panel 12: ANYONE CAN EXCHANGE GIFTS. IT TAKES A SPECIAL COUPLE TO EXCHANGE INSECURITIES.

MERRY CHRISTMAS, CATHY!

UM...THANK YOU, CHARLENE...I... UM...I'M AFRAID I LEFT YOUR GIFT AT HOME.

MERRY CHRISTMAS, CATHY.

FOR ME?...AHEM ...I...OOPS! I SEEM TO HAVE LEFT YOUR GIFT IN MY CAR...

MERRY CHRISTMAS, CATHY!

THANKS...UM ...AHEM...UM... I HAVE SOMETHING FOR YOU, TOO, BUT IT ISN'T WRAPPED.

THE HOLIDAY MAGIC CONTINUES. NOW I DON'T EVEN HAVE TO GO NEAR A STORE TO GET INTO DEBT.

THAT DOCTOR YOU MET A FEW WEEKS AGO CALLED, CATHY.

MAX CALLED?? HEAT UP THE HOT ROLLERS!

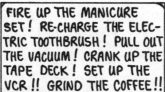

FIRE UP THE MANICURE SET! RE-CHARGE THE ELECTRIC TOOTHBRUSH! PULL OUT THE VACUUM! CRANK UP THE TAPE DECK! SET UP THE VCR!! GRIND THE COFFEE!!

PLUG IN THE IRON! RUN THE DISHWASHER!! ALERT THE MAKEUP MIRROR!!

CATHY, WHEN IRVING CALLS, YOU DON'T EVEN CHANGE YOUR SOCKS ANYMORE.

THERE'S A LOT MORE ELECTRICITY IN THE BEGINNING OF A RELATIONSHIP.

HOW AM I SUPPOSED TO TELL IRVING THAT MAX ASKED ME OUT FOR NEW YEAR'S EVE?

HOW ABOUT, "TOUGH LUCK, YOU LOSER. I GOT A BETTER OFFER"!

I DON'T ACTUALLY HAVE A DATE WITH IRVING. I JUST ASSUME THAT HE ASSUMES WE'RE DOING SOMETHING.

THEN SO WHAT? TELL HIM YOU'RE BUSY, CATHY.

IF I TELL HIM I'M BUSY, I MIGHT BE NEEDLESSLY RUBBING HIS FACE IN THE FACT THAT I HAVE A DATE. WE DON'T **KNOW** THAT HE'S PLANNING TO BE WITH ME.

I CAN'T BELIEVE THIS.

ME EITHER. BREAKING A DATE IS NOTHING COMPARED WITH BREAKING AN ASSUMPTION.

I AM NOT GOING TO ANNOUNCE THAT I'M ON A DIET THIS YEAR. I'LL JUST QUIETLY DROP THE POUNDS AND AMAZE EVERYONE!!

...I SHOULD PROBABLY EAT ONE OF THESE SO IT WON'T LOOK TO ELLEN AS IF I'M ON A DIET.

...OOPS. GRANT DIDN'T SEE ME EAT THAT ONE. I SHOULD EAT ANOTHER ONE SO HE WON'T THINK I'M ON A DIET....OOPS... SUE DIDN'T SEE ME EAT THAT ONE. I'LL HAVE TO EAT ANOTH.

HOW'S THE DIET GOING, CATHY?

YOU RUINED MY SURPRISE.

MY NEW FINANCIAL ORGANIZER...PURSE ORGANIZER...NOTE ORGANIZER...BUSINESS CARD FILE...RECEIPT FILE...APPOINTMENT BOOK...ADDRESS BOOK...

TIME PLANNER...BUDGET PLANNER...EXERCISE LOG...CALORIE CHART...DRAWER DIVIDERS... SHELF DIVIDERS... DIVIDER ORGANIZERS...PHONE INDEX...

BLEAHH!!

WE ALL DESERVE ONE LAST GASP OF SPONTANEITY.

I'M SORRY, IRVING. I ALREADY HAVE A DATE. NOT EVERY MAN WAITS UNTIL 7:30 SATURDAY NIGHT TO ASK A WOMAN OUT.

I'VE LEARNED THAT SOME MEN ARE ACTUALLY SO UNAFRAID OF COMMITMENT THAT THEY MAKE DINNER RESERVATIONS!

SOME MEN ACTUALLY SAY, "YOU LOOK BEAUTIFUL"....NOT, "WHAT'S THAT PURPLE STUFF ON YOUR EYELIDS?"!!

THERE'S NOTHING MORE DANGEROUS THAN A WOMAN WITH PERSPECTIVE.

WHAT ??

DID HE SAY HE LOVES ME ??... WHAT ??

I CAN'T ASK HIM TO REPEAT HIMSELF. IT WOULD BREAK THE WHOLE MOOD.

...BUT IF I DON'T SAY ANYTHING, HE'LL THINK I DON'T CARE AND IT WILL TAKE HIM A YEAR TO SAY IT AGAIN.

...THEN AGAIN, IF I SAY "I LOVE YOU TOO" AND HE DIDN'T SAY "I LOVE YOU," WE'LL BOTH BE EMBARRASSED. AAACK! I HAVE TO SAY SOMETHING !!

WHAT ?? DID SHE SAY SHE LOVES ME ??... WHAT ??

AN EYE FOR AN EYE, A MUMBLE FOR A MUMBLE.

I HAVE TO BE FIVE POUNDS THINNER THE NEXT TIME I SEE MAX!

STUNNING AND THINNER! THINNER! STUNNING! THIN AND STUNNING!!

I'M ADAPTING TO THE TIMES. MY DIET HAS GONE FROM A HALF-HOUR COMEDY TO A THREE-MINUTE VIDEO.

THE MAIN TEMPTATIONS USED TO BE DONUTS AND CANDY BARS. I NEEDED WILLPOWER.

... I GOT WILLPOWER, AND THEN THEY CAME OUT WITH "FAMOUS AMOS" COOKIES. THEN I NEEDED MORE WILLPOWER.

... I GOT MORE WILLPOWER, AND NOW THEY'VE INTRODUCED HOT CROISSANTS, IMPORTED ICE CREAM, HAND-DIPPED CHOCOLATES, "MRS. FIELD'S" COOKIES, CHEESECAKE PARLORS, AND A PASTA EMPORIUM ON EVERY CORNER.

EVERY NEW OUNCE OF WILL-POWER REAPS TEN NEW POUNDS OF FAT.

FEELING BETTER, CATHY?

YEAH... THIS DIET'S MAKING ME SO CRANKY, I JUST HAD TO GET SOME FRESH AIR.

THERE'S NOTHING LIKE A FEW BREATHS OF BRISK FRESH AIR TO REALLY PUT THINGS IN PERSPECTIVE!

YOU MAY WANT TO PRY THE BIG MAC BOX OFF YOUR BOOT BEFORE YOU GO INTO YOUR MEETING.

THANK YOU, CHARLENE.

I LOST THREE POUNDS?? I LOST THREE POUNDS!!

...WAIT A MINUTE. NOW IT SAYS I GAINED TWO POUNDS.

FIRST YOU FILL ME WITH HOPE AND THEN YOU SAY SOMETHING THAT RUINS EVERYTHING! WHY CAN'T YOU EVER BE CONSISTENT FOR FIVE MINUTES IN A ROW?!

THE THANKS I GET FOR TRYING TO PUT A LITTLE VARIETY IN THE RELATIONSHIP.

FOR THE FIRST TIME IN MY LIFE, MY DIET IS WORKING AND I'M READY FOR A SLEEK NEW OUTFIT!

THIS IS THE LATEST THING.

ENORMOUS, BAGGY PANTS... A GIANT SHIRT WITH PADDED SHOULDERS...

...AND OVER IT, A SHAPELESS, BULKY-KNIT SWEATER, WHICH WE WRAP WITH A JUMBO BELT AT THE HIP!!

SOME OF US ARE DOOMED TO LOOK AWESOME.

YOU MISSED A GREAT SHOE SALE, ANDREA.

I DON'T NEED MORE SHOES. I DON'T HAVE AN INSECURITY PROBLEM.

INSECURITY? HAH! I BUY SHOES IN ANTICIPATION OF THE FUTURE NEEDS OF MY BUSY, DYNAMIC LIFE!

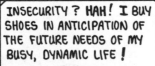

CATHY, YOU ALREADY OWN 200 PAIRS OF SHOES. WHAT COULD YOU POSSIBLY ANTICIPATE THAT ISN'T ALREADY COVERED IN HERE??

IF ANYONE EVER WANTS TO GROVEL AT MY FEET, I'M READY.

74

I HAD ONE WRINKLE. THEN MY WRINKLES CREATED THEIR OWN LITTLE WRINKLES.

I HAD ONE CHIN. THEN MY CHIN REPRODUCED ITSELF INTO MORE LITTLE CHINS.

MY SAGS CREATED LITTLE SAGS OF THEIR OWN... MY BLOTCHES CREATED LITTLE BLOTCHES...

YOU'RE THE ONLY PART OF ME THAT ISN'T PRODUCING GRANDCHILDREN.

WELL, HERE'S MY LIVING SPACE, CATHY... CONDO, SWEET CONDO!

HERE'S MY PC, MY VCR, MY WORKOUT EQUIPMENT, MY RELAXATION TANK, MY AUDIO SYSTEM, MY COMMUNICATION CENTER, MY WORK STATION....

I DON'T KNOW WHAT TO SAY, MAX.

DON'T SAY ANYTHING. I KNOW JUST WHAT YOU'RE THINKING.

THERE'S NO ROOM FOR ANY OF MY STUFF IN HERE.

IN THE '60s WE SURROUNDED OURSELVES WITH FLOWERS AND BEADS AND FELT WE HAD ALL THE ANSWERS.

IN THE '70s WE SURROUNDED OURSELVES WITH SELF-HELP BOOKS AND FELT WE HAD ALL THE ANSWERS.

IN THE '80s WE SURROUND OURSELVES WITH ELECTRONIC MACHINES AND APPLIANCES AND FEEL WE HAVE ALL THE ANSWERS.

EVERY DECADE IT GETS MORE EXPENSIVE TO BE RIGHT.

KISS..KISS..UH, MAX...YOU NEEDED TO WORK.

THE PC'S PRINTING IT.

WE'RE GOING TO MISS THE MOVIE.

THE VCR'S TAPING IT.

OUR DINNER...

THE MICROWAVE HAS IT ON HOLD.

THE PHONE...

THE ANSWERING MACHINE'S GETTING IT.

NOW WHAT'S WRONG, CATHY?

I DON'T FEEL LIKE WE'RE ALONE IN HERE.

I WANTED TO MAKE MAX JEALOUS SO I TOLD HIM I WAS SEEING IRVING.... HE SAID, "I'M PROUD OF YOU FOR CONFRONTING THOSE FEELINGS".

I WANTED TO MAKE HIM MISS ME, SO I SAID I WAS WORKING LATE....HE SAID, "I ADMIRE YOUR PROFESSIONALISM".

I WANTED TO SEDUCE HIM WITH ALOOFNESS, SO I SAID I WAS SPENDING THE WEEKEND BY MYSELF....HE SAID, "FANTASTIC. WE ALL NEED TIME TO OURSELVES."

I'VE FINALLY FOUND SOMEONE WHO'S UNDERSTANDING, AND HE'S UNDERSTANDING THE WRONG THINGS.

OKAY... I'LL BE OVER IN A LITTLE BIT, MAX.

CATHY, IT'S 8:00 AND SNOWING.

IF HE WANTS TO SEE YOU SO MUCH, WHY DIDN'T YOU TELL HIM TO JUST COME OVER HERE??

WHAT HAPPENED TO YOUR SELF-RESPECT??

SELF-RESPECT IS RELATIVE, ANDREA.

I'D RATHER DRIVE THROUGH A BLIZZARD THAN CLEAN UP MY BATHROOM.

SORRY I'M LATE, CATHY. WHILE I WAS TAPING BROKAW ON MY SONY, I RAN THE BMW 320i TO NEIMAN-MARCUS TO PICK UP SOME MAJOR GREY'S CHUTNEY.

AS SOON AS I STEPPED FOOT BACK ON MY KARASTAN, I BOOTED THE CALENDAR ON MY IBM, CHECKED MY ROLEX, JUMPED INTO MY L.L.BEANS, AND CHARGED RIGHT OVER!

WAIT, MAX... SOMETHING'S WRONG WITH YOUR JEANS POCKET.

OH, THAT'S WHERE I CUT OFF THE LABEL.

I CAN'T STAND THOSE PEOPLE WHO WALK AROUND BROAD-CASTING THE DESIGNER OF THEIR BLUE JEANS.

YOUR BAKED BRIE ALMONDINE WITH GINGERED KIWI IS IN-CREDIBLE, MAX!

THANKS. DID YOU TRY THE BASIL TORTA, CATHY?

BASIL TORTA??

...NO, CATHY. THE SMOKED YELLOWTAIL GOES WITH THE SAUCE CHIEN.

THE HOT MINT YOGURT IS FOR THE SAMOSAS.

YELLOW-TAIL? SAUCE CHIEN?

THE SAMOSAS?

YOUR CANARD PÂTÉ EVEN TOPS THE ANGEL HAIR AGLIO OLIO.

MARVELOUS PROSCIUTTO!

THE COUSCOUS WITH DILL IS HEAVEN!

AGLIO OLIO? PROSCI-UTTO? COUSCOUS?

SUDDENLY I FEEL LIKE A FAILURE AT THE ONE THING I'M GOOD AT.

WE SPENT THE FIRST 18 YEARS OF OUR LIVES WITH THEM.

I KNOW, MAX.

THEY SHAPED US, GUIDED US, ...THEY GAVE US OUR WHOLE PERSPECTIVE ON THE WORLD...

...AND NOW WE DO ALL WE CAN TO DENY THAT WE'RE STILL INFLUENCED BY THEM.

YEAH..

ARE WE TALKING ABOUT OUR PARENTS OR OUR TV SETS?

77

SO... HOW MUCH MONEY DO YOU MAKE, CATHY?

MAX, PLEASE! THIS IS ONLY OUR FIFTH DATE!

SO WHAT? LOTS OF WOMEN VOLUNTEER IT ON THE FIRST DATE.

SOME OF US STILL BELIEVE IN REALLY CARING ABOUT THE MAN BEFORE SHARING OUR FINANCES!!

IF YOU WEREN'T INTERESTED, WHY DID YOU LET ME HAVE A GLIMPSE OF YOUR AMERICAN EXPRESS CARD?!

IT'S NOT MY FAULT YOU LEAPED TO THE WRONG CONCLUSIONS!!

WE'RE NOT DOING ANY BETTER WITH THE "NEW INTIMACY" THAN WE WERE WITH THE OLD INTIMACY.

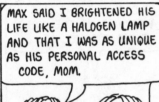

MAX SAID I BRIGHTENED HIS LIFE LIKE A HALOGEN LAMP AND THAT I WAS AS UNIQUE AS HIS PERSONAL ACCESS CODE, MOM.

HE SAID I ALREADY MEANT AS MUCH TO HIM AS PROGRAMMABLE PAUSE...

...AND THAT LIFE WITHOUT ME WOULD BE LIKE HAVING 256K OF RAM WITH NO SYSTEM DISKETTE!!

TERMS OF HIGH-TECH ENDEARMENT.

CALL THE POLICE.

THOSE ARE $150 BOOTS, MOM. I CAN'T WEAR THOSE OUTSIDE!

YOU CAN'T WEAR YOUR BOOTS OUTSIDE??

NO. I WEAR THESE OLD TENNIS SHOES OUTSIDE AND PUT ON MY BOOTS WHEN I COME INSIDE.

YOU WEAR COLD, LEAKY SHOES OUT WHERE IT'S FREEZING AND WET.... AND HOT, WATER-REPELLENT BOOTS INSIDE WHERE IT'S WARM AND DRY?

OF COURSE.

I ALWAYS HOPED THAT WHEN YOU GOT SENSIBLE, IT WOULD MAKE MORE SENSE THAN THIS.

FOR YEARS I'VE DATED IRVING, AND FOR YEARS I'VE STAYED THE SAME. SAME CLOTHES... SAME LOOK...SAME EVERYTHING.

I WAS AFRAID HE'D LOSE INTEREST IN ME IF I CHANGED A LOT.

NOW I'M DATING SOMEONE NEW WHO ENCOURAGES ME TO BE ANY WAY I WANT.

SUDDENLY I'M LOOKING AT THE WORLD THROUGH DIFFERENT EYELINER.

I CAN'T SEE YOU THIS WEEK, IRVING.

NO GOOD, CATHY. MY PARENTS ARE COMING TO TOWN. I'M COUNTING ON YOU TO BE THERE.

I CAN'T SEE YOU THIS WEEKEND.

NO GOOD. THE DALES GOT THOSE CONCERT TICKETS FOR US TWO MONTHS AGO.

I'M DATING SOMEONE ELSE, IRVING!! I CAN'T SEE YOU AT ALL!

I CAN PENCIL YOU OUT FOR THE WEEK OF THE 10TH, BUT OTHERWISE, WE HAVE A LOT OF COMMITMENTS, CATHY.

BREAKING UP IS HARD TO SCHEDULE.

CATHY...

I WOULDN'T GO IN THERE, MR. PINKLEY.

IT SEEMS THAT JUST AS CATHY'S ROMANCE WITH MAX IS PEAKING, IRVING'S PARENTS HAVE COME TO TOWN AND ACCEPTED THE DINNER INVITATION SHE EXTENDED TO THEM LAST SUMMER.

SHE'S NOW TRYING TO DECIDE HOW TO TELL HER NEW SWEETIE THAT SHE HAS TO SPEND ALL WEEK PREPARING A MEAL TO IMPRESS THE MOTHER OF THE MAN SHE PROMISED SHE WAS BREAKING UP WITH!

SOME PEOPLE HAVE RELATIONSHIPS. CATHY HAS DOCUMENTARIES.

YOU'RE CRAZY TO HAVE IRVING'S PARENTS OVER FOR DINNER JUST WHEN THINGS ARE GOING SO WELL WITH MAX.

THAT'S WHAT I THOUGHT. CRAZY.

THEN I REMEMBERED HOW GOOD I LOOK IN MY NEW JUMPSUIT.

THEN I THOUGHT, MAYBE THIS WILL BE ONE OF THOSE RICH, HUMAN EXPERIENCES THAT WILL GIVE ME A LIFE-CHANGING PERSPECTIVE ON THE WORLD!!!

CATHY, WHAT ARE YOU SAYING?

I CAN RATIONALIZE ALMOST ANYTHING IF I HAVE A CUTE OUTFIT TO WEAR FOR IT.

WHY ARE YOU CLEANING YOUR LINEN CLOSET, CATHY?? MY PARENTS ARE JUST COMING TO HAVE DINNER.

IRVING, YOU WILL "JUST BE HAVING DINNER." YOUR MOTHER WILL BE INTERVIEWING ME AS A POTENTIAL MARRIAGE CANDIDATE.

WHEN YOUR PARENTS CAME TO MY HOUSE DO YOU THINK YOUR MOTHER CHARGED OVER TO PEEK IN MY LINEN CLOSET??

DON'T BE RIDICULOUS.

FOR WOMEN CANDIDATES WE PEEK IN THE LINEN CLOSET. FOR MEN CANDIDATES, WE SNOOP THROUGH THE MEDICINE CABINET.

WHAT ARE YOU GOING TO COOK FOR MY PARENTS, CATHY?

IRVING, I'VE TOLD YOU I CAN'T COOK.

I'VE DEMONSTRATED THAT I CAN'T COOK. I'VE DONE NOTHING TO EVER INDICATE THAT I WOULD EVER BE ABLE TO COOK!!

YOU'RE A WOMAN. SOME LITTLE PART OF ME STILL SECRETLY HOPED YOU COULD COOK.

HOW COULD YOU LET HIM SAY THAT TO YOU??!

SOME LITTLE PART OF ME IS STILL SECRETLY HOPING HE'S A MILLIONAIRE.

COOKING DINNER FOR IRVING'S PARENTS IS THE FINAL GRAND GESTURE THAT WILL LET ME LEAVE THIS RELATIONSHIP GUILT-FREE, ANDREA.

HE WILL LOVE ME FOR DOING IT. HIS MOTHER WILL LOVE ME. HIS FATHER WILL LOVE ME. AND THEN I CAN DUMP HIM WITH A TOTALLY CLEAR CONSCIENCE!

CATHY, YOU'VE DATED HIM FOR SIX YEARS... AND NOW YOU'RE ENDEARING HIS ENTIRE FAMILY TO YOU TWELVE HOURS BEFORE YOU BREAK UP??!!

I DO MY MOST MEANINGFUL WORK WHEN I HAVE A DEADLINE.

I WASHED ALL THE WINDOWS, IN CASE IRVING'S MOTHER IS THE TYPE WHO INSPECTS WINDOWS.

I VACUUMED THE SOFA, STERILIZED THE SILVERWARE, POLISHED THE PLANTS, COOKED A FABULOUS MEAL, MEMORIZED THE LATEST ISSUE OF TIME, AND LEARNED TWO JOKES.

HI.

I HOPE THE SOAP IN THE BATHROOM ISN'T SCENTED. I'M ALLERGIC.

THE STORY OF MY LIFE: THE TEST IS ON THE ONE SUBJECT I DIDN'T PREPARE FOR.

YOU LOOK TIRED, IRVING. YOUR COMPANY IS TAKING ADVANTAGE OF YOU.

YOUR SUIT NEEDS PRESSING.

MOTHER, PLEASE.

YOUR MOTHER ALMOST FROZE TO DEATH TO COME VISIT YOU. DON'T SNAP AT HER.

HOW LONG COULD IT TAKE TO STOP AT THE CLEANERS??

UM... I THINK IRVING IS WONDERFUL!

YOU'D BE PRETTY IF YOU DIDN'T HAVE ALL THAT HAIR IN YOUR FACE.

YOUR COUCH IS TOO SMALL. YOUR DRAPES ARE DIRTY.

I HOPE THAT ISN'T CHEESE. I'M ALLERGIC.

ANOTHER RESCUER GOES DOWN WITH THE VICTIM.

Panel 1:
IT MUST BE WONDERFUL VISITING YOUR SON.

WE TRAVELED 1,500 MILES AND IRVING SPENDS THE WHOLE DAY AT THE OFFICE.

Panel 2:
HE HAS A GREAT JOB.

WHEN HIS FATHER WAS HIS AGE, HE OWNED FOUR STORES.

Panel 3:
I KNOW YOU'VE BOTH BEEN A BIG INSPIRATION TO HIM.

HE USED TO CALL MORE BEFORE HE SPENT SO MUCH TIME WITH YOU.

Panel 4:
HOW'S IT COMING?

DINNER WILL BE AWHILE, BUT THE PERSONALITY EXCHANGE IS COMPLETE.

Panel 5:
YOUR PARENTS HATE ME, IRVING.

YOU'RE TOO SENSITIVE, CATHY.

Panel 6:
THEY HATE MY HOME. THEY HATE MY DINNER. AND THEY HATE THAT I DATE YOU.

THAT'S JUST THE WAY THEY TALK.

Panel 7:
IF THEY DIDN'T LIKE YOU, THEY WOULDN'T TAKE THE TIME TO ATTACK YOU SO THOROUGHLY.

Panel 8:
I HAVE HEARTBURN.

I'M BLOATED.

THANK YOU.

Panel 9:
I COULD HAVE TOLD CATHY SHE WAS CRAZY TO COOK DINNER FOR IRVING'S PARENTS, BUT I SMILED AND SAID NOTHING.

Panel 10:
IF I WARNED HER, SHE'D DO IT ANYHOW AND RESENT ME. IF I SMILED AND SAID NOTHING, SHE'D DO IT AND THEN RUSH INTO MY ARMS FOR COMFORT.

Panel 11:
MOM!!

Panel 12:
I GOT THIS THE OLD-FASHIONED WAY... I CONNIVED FOR IT.

WE USED TO NOT KNOW WHAT WAS GOING ON IN OUR RELATIONSHIPS. WE GAVE EACH OTHER CARDS FOR VALENTINE'S DAY.

VALENTINE GIFT CENTER

NOW WE STILL DON'T KNOW WHAT'S GOING ON IN OUR RELATIONSHIPS.

VALENTINE GIFT CENTER

NOW WE'RE GIVING EACH OTHER DIGITAL DESK SETS, ELECTRONIC PULSE MONITORS, CELLULAR PHONES, CAPPUCCINO MAKERS, SOFTWARE, AND $150 SWEATSHIRTS FOR VALENTINE'S DAY.

1985: THE YEAR OF CONSPICUOUS CONFUSION.

WHAT?! NO VALENTINE?? WHAT?! NO CANDY?? WHAT?! NO BAUBLES??

...NO VALENTINE? I CAN'T BELIEVE IT. I DON'T KNOW WHAT TO SAY. NO VALENTINE?

AAAGH!! NO VALENTINE?! YOU SCUM! YOU THOUGHTLESS, PARANOID SCUM!!

WHAT ARE YOU DOING, CATHY? VALENTINE'S DAY ISN'T UNTIL THURSDAY.

I'M PRACTICING HOW TO LOOK SURPRISED.

VALENTINE LINGERIE

1

AAAACK!!

BAM BASH! RIIIP!! BAM CRASH!

2

IT'S HARD TO KEEP A FIGURE LIKE THIS A SECRET.

1 2

I BOUGHT YOU TWO DOZEN ROSES FOR VALENTINE'S DAY, CATHY.

OH, MAX!

THEN I THOUGHT, HOW GAUCHE. BETTER TO BRING A SINGLE, PERFECT ROSE.

OH... AHEM, WELL...

THEN I THOUGHT, HOW SUB-URBAN. BETTER TO DROP TWO INDIVIDUAL ROSE PETALS IN A SAKI CUP! FOR YOU, MY DARLING!!

AW... TEARS OF JOY.

HOW DO I EXPLAIN MINIMALISM TO MY MOTHER??

I DIDN'T DO ENOUGH FOR VALENTINE'S DAY, CHARLENE.

YOU BRIBED THE FLORIST FOR THE NAMES OF ANY-ONE THAT MAX OR IRVING SENT FLOWERS TO. ISN'T THAT ENOUGH?

I COULD HAVE BOUGHT MYSELF A GORGEOUS NECKLACE AND SAID IT WAS FROM SOMEONE ELSE... I COULD HAVE POSTED FAKE LOVE NOTES ALL OVER MY REFRIGERATOR, AND SENT MY-SELF SEVERAL BOUQUETS...

I COULD HAVE LEFT MY DATE BOOK OPEN TO A PAGE FILLED WITH PHONY DATES, AND HIRED SOMEONE TO LEAVE ROMANTIC MESSAGES ON MY MACHINE THAT MAX WOULD OVERHEAR...

YOU DID ALL YOU HAD TIME FOR, CATHY.

THERE'S NO CURSE LIKE KNOWING YOUR OWN POTENTIAL.

I'LL STAY FOR DINNER IF YOU'RE NOT HAVING JUNK FOOD, CATHY.

MAX AND I DO NOT EAT JUNK FOOD, ANDREA.

DO YOU WANT TORTELLINI-TO-GO, SUSHI-TO-GO, SZECHWAN-TO-GO, BARBECUED CHICKEN WINGS-TO-GO, TANDOORI-TO-GO...

...OR SHOULD WE JUST STICK WITH THE CHARBROILED SHRIMP BALLS ON SUGAR CANE AND TOFUTTI-TO-GO?

WE EAT JUNQUE FOOD.

MY FRIENDS ARE PAYING MORTGAGES. I PAY RENT.

MY FRIENDS ARE PAYING FOR FIVE-PHONE, TWO-LINE SYSTEMS. I PAY FOR ONE PHONE. BARE MINIMUM.

MY FRIENDS ARE PAYING FOR NEW BABY WARDROBES CHARGED ON THEIR GOLD CARDS. I'M PAYING FOR LAST YEAR'S CHRISTMAS GIFTS ON MY DEPARTMENT STORE ACCOUNT.

MY BILLS AREN'T JUST OVERDUE. THEY'RE PASSÉ.

COME ON, CATHY. THIS COULD BE PHENOMENAL BETWEEN US.

NO, MAX.

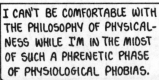

I CAN'T BE COMFORTABLE WITH THE PHILOSOPHY OF PHYSICAL-NESS WHILE I'M IN THE MIDST OF SUCH A PHRENETIC PHASE OF PHYSIOLOGICAL PHOBIAS.

WHAT ARE YOU TALKING ABOUT?

I FEEL PHAT.

MR. PINKLEY DEMANDS THAT A PROJECT BE DONE IN AN HOUR AND THEN DOESN'T LOOK AT IT FOR TWO WEEKS.

ANNOYED, I DEMAND MY DRY-CLEANING IN AN HOUR AND THEN DON'T GO BACK TO GET IT FOR TWO WEEKS.

ANNOYED, THE WOMAN FROM THE CLEANERS DEMANDS THAT HER PICTURES BE DEVELOPED IN AN HOUR, AND THEN DOESN'T PICK THEM UP FOR TWO WEEKS.

THE ECOLOGICAL CHAIN OF PHONY DEADLINES.

I WORKED FOR THREE DAYS ON DINNER FOR IRVING'S PARENTS, MAX.

"GUILT OVERCOMPENSATION." I'VE BEEN THERE, CATHY.

THEY WERE SO PICKY, I WANTED TO THROW FOOD AT THEM.

"EGO HYSTERIA". I'VE HAD THAT.

I'LL BET YOU HAVEN'T HAD "CONFRONTATIONAL REPRESSION."

HAH! I GET THAT WITH "SUCCESS ANXIETY"!

THIS WEEK ALONE, I'VE SURVIVED "TRANSITIONAL TRAUMA," "NOSTALGIA DENIAL," AND "INTROSPECTION OVERLOAD"!!

I'VE DONE ALL THAT PLUS "JEALOUSY TRANSFERENCE"!!

ARE WE BARING OUR SOULS OR COMPETING WITH THEM?

I SNEAKED OUT FOR A THREE-HOUR LUNCH WITH IRVING, AND MAX DIDN'T CALL??

MAX DIDN'T CALL, CATHY.

MAX DOESN'T EVEN KNOW I WAS OUT??

MAX DOESN'T KNOW YOU WERE OUT!

HELLO, MAX. I JUST FINISHED A THREE-HOUR LUNCH WITH IRVING AND PLAN ON SNEAKING OUT WITH HIM AGAIN TONIGHT.

WHY DID YOU DO THAT?!

SOMETIMES WE HAVE TO TAKE THE INITIATIVE IN THE RELATIONSHIP.

YOU'RE HER FATHER. YOU TELL CATHY SHE'S SPENDING TOO MUCH TIME WITH MAX.

I CAN'T TELL HER THAT.

YOU'RE HER MOTHER. YOU TELL CATHY SHE'S SPENDING TOO MUCH TIME WITH MAX.

I CAN'T TELL HER THAT.

YOU TELL CATHY SHE'S SPENDING TOO MUCH TIME WITH MAX.

I CAN'T TELL HER THAT.

WE ALWAYS STAND BEHIND EACH OTHER.

STAINLESS STEEL COOKWARE ...PASTA MAKER...SALMON POACHER...BREAD KNEADER...

VEGETABLE JUICER... FOOD PROCESSOR...TORTILLA PRESS ...COFFEE GRINDER...GELATI MAKER...COUS-COUSIER...

THERE'S STILL ONE OLD-FASHIONED KITCHEN SOUND THAT NONE OF THIS WILL EVER REPLACE, CATHY.

YEAH, I KNOW THE ONE YOU MEAN, MAX.

COOK SOMETHING !!!

I WAS A "GIRL." BY THE MID-'60s, I WAS A "WOMAN." BY THE MID-'70s, I WAS A "HUMAN BEING."

NOW WE'VE HIT THE MID-'80s, AND MY IDENTITY HAS ONCE AGAIN BEEN REDEFINED.

I AM A "CONTESTANT."

SIX MINUTES LEFT ON MY LUNCH HOUR, AND 23 SECONDS UNTIL MY CHECKS START BOUNCING...

ENDORSE ADD ADD ERASE RIP RIP SUBTRACT

SMACK!

THE SIGNATURES DON'T MATCH.

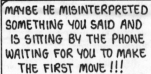

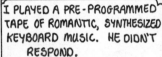

Panel 1: NO WONDER YOU'RE COLD, CATHY. WHERE ARE ALL YOUR SWEATERS? / THEY'RE FROZEN SOLID IN THE TRUNK OF MY CAR, MOM.

Panel 2: I STARTED TO TAKE THEM TO THE CLEANERS IN JANUARY... THEN I GOT BUSY... THEN I FORGOT... THEN I PUT THEM ON MY "URGENT" LIST... THEN I LOST THE LIST IN MY PURSE ...THEN I GOT BUSY....

Panel 3: WHY DON'T YOU JUST WASH THEM BY HAND? IT WOULD TAKE 15 MINUTES. / DON'T BE RIDICULOUS.

Panel 4: I ALREADY HAVE TWO AND A HALF MONTHS INVESTED IN THIS METHOD.

Panel 5: I RIDICULED MR. PINKLEY FOR GETTING A SORE THROAT... NOW I HAVE A SORE THROAT.

Panel 6: I BELITTLED JULIE FOR SUCCUMBING TO CONGESTION AND A HEADACHE... NOW I HAVE CONGESTION AND A HEADACHE.

Panel 7: I ACCUSED GRANT OF GETTING THE STOMACH FLU SO HE COULD GET OUT OF THE RINGLER PRESENTATION.... NOW I HAVE THE STOMACH FLU.

Panel 8: WHAT'S WRONG WITH CATHY? / THE PLAGUE OF SUPERIORITY.

Panel 9: I CAN'T JUST LIE HERE SICK. I SHOULD USE THIS TIME TO WRITE ALL THE LETTERS I OWE EVERYONE.

Panel 10: I SHOULD CATCH UP ON ALL MY READING... I SHOULD LIE HERE SEWING BUTTONS BACK ON THINGS...

Panel 11: I SHOULD UPDATE MY RESUME ...SET UP JOB INTERVIEWS... BALANCE MY CHECKBOOK... START MY TAXES... STUDY A FOREIGN LANGUAGE......

Panel 12: HOW ARE YOU FEELING, CATHY? / THE ONLY PART OF ME STILL FUNCTIONING IS MY STRESS.

I'M TOO SICK TO MAKE SOUP FOR MYSELF, AND YET I DROVE THROUGH A BLIZZARD SO I COULD MAKE SOUP FOR IRVING.

THE TIMES WE LEAST FEEL LIKE GIVING ARE THE TIMES IT MEANS THE MOST TO GIVE.

I DON'T EXPECT HIM TO APPRECIATE IT NOW... I ASK NOTHING IN RETURN... IT IS A PURE AND SIMPLE SHOW OF UNSELFISH LOVE !!

SOMEWHERE BETWEEN THE POTATOES AND THE CHICKENS, I TURNED INTO MY MOTHER.

I'VE BEEN LYING HERE ON THE BRINK OF DEATH, AND YOU'VE BEEN RUNNING AROUND WITH SOME OTHER GUY !!

WE'LL TALK WHEN YOU'RE FEELING BETTER.

I BROUGHT YOU SOME CHICK—...WAIT A MINUTE. THERE'S ALREADY CHICKEN SOUP IN HERE !

I'VE BEEN TRYING TO PUT YOU OUT OF MY MIND, AND YOU'VE BEEN EATING ANOTHER WOMAN'S CHICKEN SOUP !!

WE'LL TALK WHEN YOU'RE FEELING BETTER, CATHY.

HOW'S IRVING ?

HE'S VERY CONTAGIOUS.

GLENDALE APARTMENTS

"TO HELP FIGHT THE 'FLU BLAHS' CURL UP IN A COMFY FLANNEL NIGHTSHIRT AND FLUFFY SLIPPERS, AND TIE HAIR UP WITH BRIGHT RIBBONS...."

"PAMPER YOURSELF WITH A SOOTHING BUBBLE BATH AND HERBAL FACE MASK WHILE SIPPING STEAMY BROTH FROM A CHEERY CERAMIC MUG...."

WHAT IS THE MATTER WITH YOU ?? CAN'T I EVEN BE SICK WITHOUT WORRYING ABOUT LOOKING "PERKY"?!!

...."TO SOOTHE A SPRAINED WRIST, WRAP IN A COLORFUL BANDANA, AND COORDINATE WITH KICKY PINK LEGWARMERS..."

I'M TOO SICK TO WORK. I'M TOO SICK TO READ. I'M TOO SICK TO WATCH TV. I'M TOO SICK TO CALL ANYONE.

I'M TOO SICK TO THINK. I'M TOO SICK TO WASH MY FACE. I'M TOO SICK TO GET DRESSED. I'M TOO SICK TO MOVE.

AND YET I HAVE THE ENERGY TO RUN IN AND LEAP ON THE SCALE EVERY 15 MINUTES TO SEE IF I'M LOSING WEIGHT.

WE ALWAYS FIND THE STRENGTH TO DO THE ONE THING THAT WILL MAKE US FEEL WORSE.

I WANT MY SOUP BACK, IRVING.

I'M TOO SICK TO BRING YOU SOUP, CATHY.

BESIDES, I GAVE YOUR SOUP TO JULIE, WHO GOT SICK WHEN SHE WAS TAKING SOUP TO TOM.

WHEN TOM WAS TAKING SOUP TO CHRIS HE RAN INTO CHARLENE, WHO WAS TAKING SOUP TO JIM. JIM HAD ALREADY SENT SOUP TO BARB, WHO SAID AS SOON AS SHE'S BETTER, SHE'LL BRING SOUP TO YOU.

I'M NO LONGER A PERSON. I'M JUST A LINK IN THE SOUP EXCHANGE.

MY SWEETIE... MY DOCTOR... YOU'VE COME TO CURE ME!

WHY ARE YOU IN YOUR ROBE? OUR AEROBICS CLASS STARTS IN 10 MINUTES!

MAX, I'M SICK.

SICK?? OUR GENERATION DOESN'T GET SICK, CATHY!

WE EAT THE FINEST FOODS... WE CHECK OUR BIORHYTHMS... WE DRIVE $25,000 CARS AND ADORN OUR PERFECT MUSCLE TONE IN DESIGNER LABELS... BUT WE DO NOT GET SICK!!!

WHY NOT?

IT SEEMS SO SELF-INDULGENT.

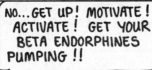

WELCOME BACK, CATHY. WHAT DID YOU BUY?

I HAD THE FLU, CHARLENE. I WAS NOT SHOPPING!

SURE, YOU HAD THE FLU FOR A WHILE, BUT EVERYONE FAKES IT THE LAST FEW DAYS AND GOES SHOPPING.

I AM A PROFESSIONAL, CHARLENE! I RETURNED TO WORK THE SECOND I RECOVERED!

.... THE SECOND I RE-COVERED MY FEET WITH NEW SHOES... AND RE-COVERED THE REST OF ME WITH NEW OUTFITS.

I THOUGHT MORRIE WAS DOING ALL MY WORK WHILE I WAS SICK.

OH. MORRIE GOT SICK AND GAVE YOUR WORK AND HIS TO ELLEN.

ELLEN GOT SICK AND GAVE YOURS, MORRIE'S AND HER WORK TO GRANT... GRANT GOT SICK AND GAVE YOURS MORRIE'S, ELLEN'S AND HIS WORK TO JACK...

JACK GOT SICK AND TURNED THE ENTIRE COMPANY'S WORK BACK OVER TO YOU.

NOT MANY OFFICES COULD TURN PROCRASTINATION INTO AN EPIDEMIC.

I'D BETTER GET GOING. MY HUSBAND IS TAKING ME TO THE SYMPHONY TONIGHT!

I HAVE TO RUN, TOO. MY HUSBAND IS COOKING ME A FABULOUS MEAL!

WELL, I, TOO, HAVE SOMEONE WAITING AT HOME FULL OF ROMANCE, HUMOR, ENTERTAINMENT AND SURPRISES!!

HER VCR'S BEEN TAPING MOVIES ALL DAY.

WE CHERISH WHAT WE HAVE.

Panel 1: GRANT AND I WERE STILL WORKING ON THE REESE FIGURES AT 9:15... GRANT? IS HE STILL UNATTACHED?

Panel 2: MOTHER, PLEASE. ...ANYWAY, BOB REESE GOT THERE AT 9:30 AND... BOB?? IS HE SINGLE?? DO YOU LIKE HIM?

Panel 3: WAITER, PLEASE BRING THE CHECK! WAITER?? IS HE WEARING A RING? DO YOU THINK HE'S CUTE?

Panel 4: MOTHERS DON'T SETTLE DOWN UNTIL THE DAUGHTERS SETTLE DOWN.

Panel 5: IRVING WILL NEVER OPEN UP TO ME, MAX. TOO BAD. THAT'S HIS LOSS.

Panel 6: WILL YOU OPEN UP TO ME? THE RISK-TAKING INVOLVED IN A PRIMARY RELATIONSHIP IS AN EXHILARATION I LIVE FOR, CATHY!

Panel 7: WILL YOU OPEN UP TO ME NOW? YES! I BELIEVE IN THE CONSTANT REASSESSMENT OF EMOTIONAL INTIMACY! YES! I WILL ALWAYS BE AS OPEN WITH YOU AS I AM NOW!

Panel 8: THE '80s RELATIONSHIP: PEDALING HARDER, STILL GOING NOWHERE.

Panel 9: I'VE BEEN PAYING FOR TWO YEARS, AND I STILL OWE $7,000 ON MY $6,000 CAR?!

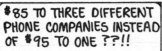

Panel 10: $85 TO THREE DIFFERENT PHONE COMPANIES INSTEAD OF $95 TO ONE??!! BAM

Panel 11: $150 TO KEEP THIS MISERABLE APARTMENT AT THE TEMPERATURE REQUIRED TO CATCH PNEUMONIA! HAH. BAM BAM BAM

Panel 12: IN OUR OWN WAY, WE'RE ALL PARTICIPATING IN THE ECONOMIC UPSWING.

97

ON SATURDAY I SAW MAX. I FELT EXHILARATED. I CAME HOME AND ATE.

ON SUNDAY I SAW IRVING. I FELT GUILTY. I CAME HOME AND ATE.

TODAY I SAW NO ONE AND FELT NOTHING. I CAME HOME AND ATE.

I GUESS THIS SORT OF NARROWS DOWN THE SOURCE OF THE PROBLEM, CATHY.

MY HOME IS MAKING ME FAT!!

7:01AM: THE WAR ON FAT HAS BEGUN!

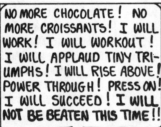 

NO MORE CHOCOLATE! NO MORE CROISSANTS! I WILL WORK! I WILL WORKOUT! I WILL APPLAUD TINY TRIUMPHS! I WILL RISE ABOVE! POWER THROUGH! PRESS ON! I WILL SUCCEED! I WILL NOT BE BEATEN THIS TIME!!

7:02AM: ONCE AGAIN, I'VE EXHAUSTED ALL MY AMMUNITION IN THE FIRST SIXTY SECONDS OF BATTLE.

JUST A SALAD. I'M ON A DIET.

OH YEAH? HOW MUCH WEIGHT HAVE YOU LOST, CATHY?

THIS IS A NEW DIET, CHARLENE... ...AN EATING PROGRAM FOR THE REST OF MY LIFE!

YOU HAVEN'T LOST ANY WEIGHT YET?

CHARLENE, I'VE ONLY BEEN ON THE DIET FOR 3 HOURS!! DON'T MAKE ME FEEL LIKE I'VE ALREADY FAILED BECAUSE I DON'T HAVE ANY BIG NUMBERS TO REPORT YET!!

YOU'LL HAVE TO EXCUSE HER. SHE'S ON A DIET.

OH YEAH? HOW MUCH WEIGHT HAS SHE LOST?

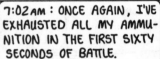

9:00am: I'VE CONVINCED MY-SELF I CAN'T RETURN ANY PHONE CALLS WITHOUT FIRST EATING A DONUT.

9:15am: I'VE CONVINCED MY-SELF THAT I NOT ONLY CAN'T RETURN CALLS, BUT I CAN'T READ THESE MEMOS WITHOUT FIRST EATING A DONUT.

9:30am: I'VE NOW CONVINCED MYSELF THAT MY ENTIRE FUTURE WITH THIS CORPORATION DEPENDS ON MY ABILITY TO FIND AND EAT A DONUT.

WE'RE NEVER PREPARED FOR WHERE OUR CAREERS MIGHT TAKE US.

I COULD HAVE HAD A TINY FRUIT CUP FOR LUNCH, BUT NO. I ORDERED A VAT OF PASTA SALAD.

I COULD HAVE NIBBLED ON A BREADSTICK, BUT NO. I HAD A CROISSANT SMEARED WITH BUTTER AND JAM.

I COULD HAVE HAD A CUP OF BLACK COFFEE, BUT NO. I INSISTED ON CAPPUCCINO AND ADDED TWO SPOONS OF SUGAR.

WHAT'S GOING ON, CATHY? — I'M EXERCISING MY OPTIONS.

I WAS DOING PERFECTLY ON MY DIET, AND THEN I THOUGHT, WHAT'S THE POINT? I'M JUST GOING TO BLOW IT ON EASTER CANDY.

EASTER CANDY

THEN I THOUGHT, IF I DON'T BLOW IT ON EASTER, I'LL DEFINITELY EAT MY WAY THROUGH MEMORIAL DAY AND THE FOURTH OF JULY.

THEN I THOUGHT, EVEN IF I DON'T BLOW IT THIS SUMMER, I'LL NEVER GET THROUGH HALLOWEEN, THANKSGIVING, AND THE HOLIDAY SEASON....

BAKERY

THE ONLY THING I EVER DO AHEAD OF TIME FOR CHRISTMAS IS CHEAT ON MY DIET

I WOKE UP THINKING ABOUT CHOCOLATE. I THOUGHT ABOUT CHOCOLATE ALL DAY.

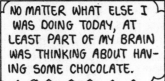

NO MATTER WHAT ELSE I WAS DOING TODAY, AT LEAST PART OF MY BRAIN WAS THINKING ABOUT HAVING SOME CHOCOLATE.

I FOUGHT AND WON 10,000 BATTLES AGAINST CHOCOLATE TODAY! I LIVED THROUGH THE DAY AND DID NOT EAT ANY CHOCOLATE!!

HOW'D IT GO TODAY, CATHY?

THE ONE THIN ACCOMPLISHED I'M REALLY PR OF SOUNDS TO STUPID TO TELL ANYONE.

WASN'T IRVING SUPPOSED TO BE HERE AT 7:00?

YES. BUT NOW HE'LL HAVE TO SPEND BETWEEN 7:15 AND 7:30 MAKING EXCUSES FOR BEING LATE.

BETWEEN 7:30 AND 7:45, HE'LL BE ANNOYED WITH HIMSELF FOR FEELING HE'S SUPPOSED TO HAVE AN EXPLANATION.

AND THEN HE'LL SPEND BETWEEN 7:45 AND 8:15 FIGURING A WAY TO TWIST THE SITUATION SO I'LL FEEL STUPID IF I MAKE A BIG DEAL OUT OF IT.

SOMETIMES IT HELPS TO KNOW A MAN'S SCHEDULE, SOMETIMES IT DOESN'T.

I SHOULD HAVE LET MYSELF HAVE A TASTE OF THAT PIE AT DINNER.

YOU'VE BEEN TALKING ABOUT THAT PIE FOR FOUR HOURS, CATHY.

IRVING, THE SAME PERSONAL-ITY TRAIT THAT MAKES IT POSSIBLE FOR ME TO FIXATE ON ONE BITE OF PIE FOR THREE WEEKS HAS MADE IT POSSIBLE FOR ME TO STAY FASCINATED WITH YOU FOR SIX YEARS!!!

YOU SHOULD THANK YOUR LUCKY STARS I'M THE TYPE OF WOMAN WHO CAN SUS-TAIN THIS KIND OF OBSESSION!

WHAT WE LACK IN MEANING-FUL DIALOGUES, WE MAKE UP FOR IN MEANINGFUL MONOLOGUES.

SLAM!

I'VE TORTURED MYSELF FOR MONTHS ABOUT THE LETTERS I OWE PEOPLE... WHEN JAN OWES LETTERS, SHE JUST SAYS, "OOPS. HA, HA! I'M SUCH A PROCRASTINATOR!"

I AGONIZED FOR WEEKS OVER LETTING THIS PROJECT SLIDE... WHEN GRANT DID THE SAME THING, HE JUST SAID, "OOPS. HA, HA! WIN SOME, LOSE SOME."

I TOTALLY BERATED MYSELF FOR EATING ONE CRACKER THAT WASN'T ON MY DIET... CHARLENE ATE A CHEESECAKE AND SAID, "OOPS. HA, HA! BETTER LUCK TOMORROW!"

THE ONLY PEOPLE WHO AREN'T SUCCEEDING BETTER THAN I AM ARE FAILING BETTER THAN I AM.

ONE TINY TASTE OF CRUMB-CAKE IS **NOT** GOING TO RUIN MY WHOLE DIET.

ONE TINY TASTE OF CRUMB-CAKE AND ONE MINUSCULE BAG OF CHIPS IS **NOT** GOING TO RUIN MY DIET.

A TINY CRUMBCAKE, A FEW CHIPS... A SMALL SANDWICH... MICROWAVE POP-CORN! BROWNIES! GUACAMOLE AND M&M'S!!!

WHAT ARE YOU DOING, CATHY?!

THE STORY OF MY LIFE: I STARTED PLANNING A LITTLE SNACK, AND IT TURNED INTO A DINNER PARTY.

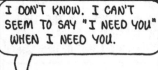

I NEEDED YOU LAST WEEK, MAX.

WHY DIDN'T YOU TELL ME THAT LAST WEEK?

I DON'T KNOW. I CAN'T SEEM TO SAY "I NEED YOU" WHEN I NEED YOU.

I CAN ONLY SAY "I NEEDED YOU" AFTER THE CRISIS IS OVER.

IF YOU CAN'T SAY YOU NEED ME NOW, WHY CAN YOU SAY YOU NEEDED ME LAST WEEK?

IT SOUNDS LIKE I WAS YOUNGER THEN.

I CAN'T ASK MY BOYFRIEND ABOUT MY TAXES BECAUSE I DON'T WANT HIM TO SEE HOW LITTLE I MAKE...

I CAN'T ASK DAD ABOUT MY TAXES BECAUSE I DON'T WANT HIM TO SEE HOW MUCH I MAKE.... I CAN'T ASK A PROFESSIONAL BECAUSE I DON'T WANT ANYONE TO SEE HOW DISORGANIZED I AM...

THIS YEAR I WILL DO MY TAXES ENTIRELY BY MYSELF !!!

SOMETIMES IT'S HARD TO KNOW IF I'M INDEPENDENT OR JUST EMBARRASSED.

SO WHAT IF I HAVE TO DEAL WITH AN ENTIRE YEAR OF FINANCES IN SIX DAYS ? AT LEAST I HAVE SIX DAYS.

SIX DAYS... A SIX-PACK OF DIET POP...AND SIX MONTHS OF NEWSPAPERS AND MAGAZINES FILLED WITH ALL THE ADVICE I'VE BEEN IGNORING.

I'LL READ UP ON TAX SHELTERS... snip snip!... COMPARE IRAs ...snip snip!... STUDY TAX SERVICES...snip snip... ANALYZE MY OPTIONS...snip! snip! ORGANIZE !..snip!.. FILE ! INVEST ! DEFER !!

SNIP! SNIP! SNIP SNIP. SNIP

...ONE OPTIMISTIC MOMENT REAPS 200 POUNDS OF GARBAGE.

IF YOU ASK ME IF I'VE OPENED MY IRA YET AGAIN, DAD, I'LL SCREAM.

I AM A GROWN WOMAN. I DO NOT NEED YOUR ANNUAL LECTURE ON IRAs. DON'T EVEN MENTION IRAs, DAD. I WILL NOT DISCUSS MY IRA.

NO, I DID NOT OPEN MY IRA YET, BUT YES, I'M GOING TO !!!

THAT WAS VERY GOOD, DEAR!

WHO SAYS THAT ONLY MOTHERS CAN COMMUNICATE WITH THEIR DAUGHTERS ?

Row 1:

IF I MAIL MY CHECK TO THE I.R.S. AT THE LAST SECOND TONIGHT, IT WILL GET THERE IN 48-52 HOURS...

...PLUS FOUR DAYS FOR SORTING AND OPENING... THREE FOR RECORDING AND DEPOSITING... THREE FOR GETTING BACK TO MY BANK...

....IF EVERYTHING BREAKS MY WAY, I COULD HAVE UP TO 12½ DAYS TO GET MONEY INTO MY ACCOUNT BEFORE MY CHECK BOUNCES !!

INCREDIBLE.

I KNOW. THIS IS THE ONE AREA WHERE MY PREVIOUS FINANCIAL EXPERIENCE CAN REALLY PAY OFF.

Row 2:

ATTENTION ALL EMPLOYEES: ON THIS DAY AFTER TAX DAY, EACH OF US IS COPING WITH FINANCIAL RUIN IN HIS OWN WAY.

SOME OF US ARE QUIETLY TORTURING OURSELVES... SOME ARE TURNING OUR DEPRESSION INTO STRENGTH TO EXCEL....

AS YOUR CARING EMPLOYER, I WANT TO THANK YOU FOR ENDURING LAST YEAR'S CUTBACKS, AND REASSURE YOU THAT NO MATTER HOW YOU'RE DIRECTING YOUR FRUSTRATION, YOU ARE NOT ALONE !!

...UNFORTUNATELY.

Row 3:

I NEED A FULL, WRITTEN RECEIPT INCLUDING DATE, AMOUNT, PURPOSE AND WITNESSES, WHICH I WILL RECORD IN MY RECEIPT LOG !

CATHY, THE FIRST RECEIPT YOU GET AFTER TAX DAY GETS SAVED, LOGGED, BUDGETED, STAPLED, PHOTOCOPIED, FILED, STAMPED, ENSHRINED AND GLOATED OVER.

....EVERY OTHER RECEIPT ALL YEAR GETS WADDED UP IN THE BOTTOM OF YOUR PURSE !

LIFE IS GOOD TO THE FIRST BORN, ANDREA.

Panel 1: I JUST WANT ONE NORMAL WEEK. IS THAT SO MUCH TO ASK?

Panel 2: ...JUST ONE NORMAL WEEK WHERE I HAVE NORMAL, NON-HYSTERICAL WORK DAYS, AND COME HOME TO A NORMAL, NON-CRISIS-POINT RELATIONSHIP.

Panel 3: I'VE NEVER HAD A WEEK LIKE THAT. ME EITHER. ME EITHER.

Panel 4: WHY DOES THE ONE EXPERIENCE NO ONE HAS EVER HAD KEEP SEEMING LIKE THE NORMAL ONE?

Panel 5: THIS SUIT LOOKS OLD AND DATED, BUT I CAN'T AFFORD A NEW ONE. THE MEN IN MY POSITION WEAR EXPENSIVE NEW SUITS ALL THE TIME!

Panel 6: THE MEN IN MY POSITION ARE BUYING HOUSES AND CARS, AND I STILL DON'T MAKE ENOUGH TO BUY THE KIND OF CLOTHES I SHOULD BE WEARING!!

Panel 7: MR. PINKLEY, WE'RE DISCUSSING MY RAISE TODAY AND THAT'S ALL THERE IS TO IT!!

Panel 8: NEVER UNDERESTIMATE THE POWER OF THE WRONG OUTFIT.

Panel 12: THE FASHION INDUSTRY HAS FINALLY DONE IT, CHARLENE. I CAN'T TELL THE "BEFORES" FROM THE "AFTERS."

106

I USE DEODORANT AND GET A CHANCE TO WIN A MILLION DOLLARS... I EAT BREAKFAST, AND COULD WIN A MILLION DOLLARS...

I DO THE LAUNDRY, COULD WIN A MILLION DOLLARS... WASH MY FACE, COULD WIN A MILLION DOLLARS... TAKE OUT THE GARBAGE, COULD WIN A MILLION DOLLARS....

NO WONDER I'M LOSING MY ENTHUSIASM FOR GOING TO WORK.

IT'S THE ONLY THING I DO WITH NO POTENTIAL FOR MAKING ANY MONEY.

IF YOU GET YOUR RAISE TODAY, CATHY, I'LL BE SO EXCITED AND PROUD OF YOU.

THANK YOU, MAX.

IF YOU DON'T GET YOUR RAISE, I'LL BE SUPPORTIVE AND UNDERSTANDING.

THANK YOU, MAX.

I WANT YOU TO GO INTO THAT OFFICE WITH ONLY ONE THING ON YOUR MIND !!

WILL I GET A BETTER HUG IF I FAIL OR IF I SUCCEED?

PRODUCT TESTING INC.

I WANT THIS RAISE BECAUSE I WANT TO SEE MAX'S AUBURN EYES SPARKLE IN THE MOONLIGHT WHEN I TELL HIM ABOUT IT !

CHECK.

I WANT THIS RAISE SO I CAN BUY A $20,000 CONVERTIBLE, DRIVE BY IRVING'S APARTMENT AND MAKE HIM JEALOUS !

CHECK.

I WANT THIS RAISE SO I CAN STUFF MYSELF WITH CHOCOLATE IN SOME COUNTRY SO FAR AWAY THAT NO ONE CAN SEE HOW FAT I GET !

CHECK. ....CATHY'S READY TO SEE YOU NOW, MR. PINKLEY.

THANKS, CHARLENE. I DO BETTER IN NEGOTIATIONS IF I GET THE TRUTH OUT OF MY SYSTEM FIRST.

HI. WHERE IS EVERYONE?

SUE'S IN A MEETING, GRANT'S IN CONFERENCE, AND YOUR MENTOR IS HIDING IN THE MEN'S ROOM.

PRODUCT TESTING INC.

GET OUT OF THERE, YOU COWARD! YOU PROMISED TO RE-DISCUSS MY RAISE TODAY!

I'LL RE-DISCUSS YOUR RAISE WHEN YOU SHOW ME THE 200-PAGE REPORT YOU PROMISED LAST MONTH!

BAM BAM

MEN

MEN

AT LAST... A PROTÉGÉE WHO REALLY FOLLOWS MY EXAMPLE!

WOMEN

FOR FIVE YEARS, ALL I'VE DONE TO MAKE MORE MONEY IS PICK AT MR. PINKLEY FOR A RAISE. I PICK... I GIVE UP. I PICK... I GIVE UP.

TODAY I WAS SO FURIOUS THAT I UPDATED MY RESUME, SIGNED UP WITH A HEAD-HUNTER, SCHEDULED INTERVIEWS AND BOOKED FLIGHTS, ALL DURING MY LUNCH HOUR.

MOM WAS RIGHT.

ONE HOT LUNCH IS MORE SATISFYING THAN LOTS OF LITTLE SNACKS.

WHAT DO YOU MEAN, YOU'RE INTERVIEWING SOMEWHERE ELSE, CATHY?

I'M THROUGH BEGGING YOU FOR MONEY AND RESPECT, MR. PINKLEY.

PINKLEY

OH, COME ON... WE CAN DISCUSS IT...

THERE'S NOTHING LEFT TO DISCUSS. WHEN I BREAK UP, MR. PINKLEY, I BREAK UP!!

HA HA HA HOO HA HA HA!!

IT'S HARD TO HAVE CREDIBILITY WHEN THE ENTIRE OFFICE KNOWS THE HISTORY OF YOUR LOVE LIFE.

YOU WOULDN'T CARE IF I TOOK A JOB 2500 MILES AWAY, MAX??

DISTANCE DOESN'T HAVE TO CHANGE A RELATIONSHIP ANYMORE, CATHY.

...HE'S GOING INTO THE KITCHEN TO CALL ANOTHER WOMAN.....HE'S SNEAKING IN THERE TO HIDE SOMETHING.....

HE HAS ANOTHER WOMAN HIDDEN IN THE KITCHEN AND THEY'RE STANDING IN THERE LAUGHING ABOUT ME.

DO YOU THINK DISTANCE WOULD CHANGE OUR RELATIONSHIP?

PROBABLY NOT.

YOU'LL HAVE TO CALL YOUR COUSIN TOM WHEN YOU'RE IN CALIFORNIA, CATHY.

MOM, THIS IS A BUSINESS TRIP!

THE JOHNSTONS WOULD BE CRUSHED IF YOU CAME TO TOWN WITHOUT STOPPING BY.

MOM, I'M FLYING ACROSS THE COUNTRY FOR A ONE-DAY INTERVIEW THAT COULD CHANGE MY ENTIRE CAREER! ONLY ONE THING MATTERS!!

I HAVE TO COME HOME WITH A SUNTAN.

I'LL TAKE MY SUIT TO THE STORE SO I CAN FIND A NEW BLOUSE TO MATCH IT FOR MY INTERVIEW.

IN CASE I CAN'T FIND A NEW BLOUSE, I'LL TAKE MY OLD BLOUSE AND LOOK FOR SHOES TO MATCH.

IN CASE I CAN'T FIND NEW SHOES I'LL BRING MY OLD SHOES AND LOOK FOR EARRINGS TO MATCH...OR MAYBE A NECKLACE FOR THIS SWEATER...OR MAYBE I'LL BUILD A WHOLE OUTFIT AROUND THIS DRESS...

MAY I HELP YOU?

YES. I'M LOOKING FOR SOMETHING TO WEAR.

SPRING FASHION

A SIZE 11 BODY PACKED INTO A SIZE 9 SKIRT...SIZE 7 FEET CRAMMED INTO SIZE 6 SHOES.

TWO WEEKS OF CLOTHES STUFFED INTO AN OVERNIGHT BAG...AN ENTIRE BATHROOM SQUASHED INTO A PURSE.

FIVE YEARS OF EMOTION WADDED UP INTO ONE DESPERATE GLANCE.

YOU CAN'T GET ALL THAT INTO THAT LITTLE SPACE, MISS.

YOU DON'T KNOW WHO YOU'RE DEALING WITH.

I'M FLYING 2,500 MILES FROM EVERYONE I LOVE FOR A JOB INTERVIEW.....SHE'S TAKING HER SQUALLING BABY TO MEET ITS GRANDPARENTS.

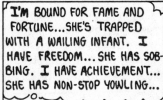

I'M BOUND FOR FAME AND FORTUNE...SHE'S TRAPPED WITH A WAILING INFANT. I HAVE FREEDOM...SHE HAS SOBBING. I HAVE ACHIEVEMENT... SHE HAS NON-STOP YOWLING...

I HAVE TO CHANGE SEATS. THE BABY NEXT TO ME ISN'T SCREAMING ENOUGH.

KNOW WHAT MAKES THIS COMPANY SO SPECIAL, CATHY? COMMITMENT! KNOW WHY PEOPLE ARE HERE WORKING THIS LATE AT NIGHT? COMMITMENT!

KNOW WHAT WE SAW IN YOUR RESUME? COMMITMENT! YOU BELIEVE LIKE WE DO THAT WHEN YOU START SOMETHING, YOU SEE IT THROUGH TO THE END !!

"DYNASTY'S" TWO-PART SEASON FINALE STARTS IN FIFTEEN MINUTES !!

I FIT RIGHT IN.

HELLO. THIS IS ROOM 822. ANY MESSAGES?

NO MESSAGES. WAS YOUR LITTLE LIGHT BLINKING?

I THOUGHT MY LITTLE LIGHT MIGHT BE BROKEN. I WAS **SURE** I'D HAVE A MESSAGE.

HAVE YOU DONE ANYTHING TO DESERVE A MESSAGE? HAVE YOU CALLED HIM? HAVE YOU TOLD HIM YOU CARE??

HAVE YOU TAKEN AN ACTIVE ROLE IN THE AFFAIRS OF YOUR HEART, OR HAVE YOU GOTTEN SO LAZY THAT YOU'VE DISCOURAGED THE LITTLE LIGHT FROM EVEN COMING ON, LET ALONE BLINKING??

I MISS MY ANSWERING MACHINE.

WE'LL TALK SOON, CATHY. HERE'S MY CARD.

TAKE MY CARD TOO, IN CASE YOU HAVE QUESTIONS.

HERE'S MY CARD IN CASE HE ISN'T IN.

OH, AND SEND YOUR EXPENSES TO ME. HERE'S MY CARD.

TAKE MY CARD, TOO. I'D LOVE TO HAVE LUNCH.

WAIT...HERE'S MY CARD.

MY CARD....

THANK YOU. IT WAS WONDERFUL TO MEET ALL OF YOU. I'LL BE IN TOUCH. THANK YOU...

WHO **ARE** ALL THESE PEOPLE?

MAYBE THE MAN I SAW ON THE WAY TO MY INTERVIEW WILL BE IN THE RESTAURANT... MAYBE HE'S HOPING TO RUN INTO ME.....

PRIMP
FLUFF
SQUIRT
PRIMP

HI YA, SWEETIE! WANT SOME COMPANY??

NO, I MOST CERTAINLY DO NOT WANT COMPANY!

THAT'S THE PROBLEM WITH EATING ALONE... THE WRONG PERSON ALWAYS THINKS YOU'RE JUST THERE TO GET PICKED UP.

cathy by Cathy Guisewite

DUE OVERDUE

WE WANT YOUR IDEAS, YOUR THOUGHTS, YOUR FEELINGS...

...WE'RE MORE DESPERATE THIS WEEK THAN USUAL.

DUE

DUE OVERDUE

NOW, THEN... IS IT BETTER TO DO THE MOST RECENT ASSIGNMENT FIRST AND PUT OFF THE THINGS THAT ARE ALREADY OVERDUE, MAKING ONE THING GET DONE ON TIME?

DUE OVERDUE

OR IS IT BETTER TO DO THE OVERDUE THINGS FIRST AND PUT OFF THE NEW ASSIGNMENT SO EVERYTHING LEVELS OFF TO ONE UNIFORM LATENESS?

WHY DON'T WE HIRE MORE PEOPLE SO WE DON'T KEEP TRYING TO GET 25,000 HOURS OF WORK OUT OF TEN EMPLOYEES EVERY WEEK??

DUE OVERDUE

YEA! BRAVO! YEA! WHISTLE WHISTLE YAAA! BRAVO!

OVERDUE

THIS CONCLUDES THE "STAFF OPINION" PORTION OF THE MEETING.

I'D LOVE FOR YOU TO COME OVER, CATHY, BUT YOU MUST BE EXHAUSTED FROM YOUR TRIP.

OH, I'M NOT AS TIRED AS I THOUGHT I'D BE, MAX...

IF YOU JUST WANT TO STAY THERE, I UNDERSTAND.

HO, HUM... WELL, I MIGHT STOP BY FOR A FEW MINUTES.

I CAN'T BELIEVE THIS, CATHY! WHAT MAN WOULD JUMP OFF AN AIRPLANE AND GO RACING OVER TO VISIT HIS GIRLFRIEND ??!

WHAT MAN WOULD HAVE SPENT THE WHOLE TRIP HOME TRYING TO SHAVE HIS LEGS IN THE AIRPLANE BATHROOM?

I'LL TELL MR. PINKLEY MY INTERVIEW WAS GREAT AND THAT I'M REALLY CONSIDERING THEIR OFFER...

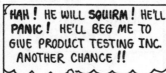

HAH! HE WILL SQUIRM! HE'LL PANIC! HE'LL BEG ME TO GIVE PRODUCT TESTING INC. ANOTHER CHANCE!!

I'M BACK! THEY WERE TERRIBLE! YOU DIDN'T GIVE MY JOB AWAY, DID YOU ??!

...AND I WONDER WHY MY DATES NEVER GET JEALOUS...

WHERE'S YOUR BARBE-CUE, CATHY?

I LOST IT THE LAST TIME I BROKE UP WITH IRVING....

...BUT I GOT CUSTODY OF THIS HIBACHI WHEN I BROKE UP WITH PAUL. I HAD TO GIVE UP THE PICNIC SET WHEN I BROKE UP WITH BRIAN....

...BUT I GOT TO KEEP THE SAL-AD BOWLS WHEN I BROKE UP WITH JAKE...3 MUGS WHEN I BROKE UP WITH BILL...AND 47 PLASTIC GLASSES WHEN I BROKE UP WITH GRANT.

I'VE BEEN THROUGH A LOT OF DIVORCES FOR SOMEONE WHO'S NEVER BEEN MARRIED.

HELLO, IS MAX IN, PLEASE?

CATHY.

WHO SHALL I SAY IS CALLING?

CATHY....??

I'M A FRIEND. HE'LL KNOW.

ONE MOMENT. I'LL PAGE HIM FOR YOU.

AACK! NO! DON'T PAGE HIM! WAIT!! AACK! FORGET THE CALL! RIP UP MY NAME! AAACK!!

OUR RELATIONSHIP JUST FLUNKED THE PAGING TEST.

I SAW THIS COLOGNE IN AN AD, CHARLENE. IT'S PERFECT FOR ME!!

I LOVE THE NAME... I LOVE THE BOTTLE... I LOVE THE PACKAGING... THIS COLOGNE SUMS UP WHO I AM AND WHAT I NOW WANT FROM LIFE!!

SQUIRT!

...BLEAH! THAT'S IT?? BLEAH!!

WIPE RUB WIPE

NOW WHAT AM I SUPPOSED TO DO? MY NEW IMAGE STINKS.

ARE YOU GOING TO GO ON MORE INTERVIEWS, CATHY?

ABSOLUTELY. IT'S MY NEW ATTITUDE, CHARLENE.

WHEN YOU'RE CLOSED TO NEW OPPORTUNITIES, NOTHING HAPPENS.

COFFEE RO

BUT WHEN YOU OPEN UP ONE LITTLE PART OF YOUR LIFE TO NEW OPPORTUNITIES, SUDDENLY EACH AND EVERY PART OF YOUR LIFE IS FILLED WITH NEW OPPORTUNITIES!!

JUST MY LUCK. THE FIRST THING I RAN INTO WAS A CHOCOLATE ÉCLAIR.

116

I'LL SUN WITH MY STRAPS UP. NO. DOWN. NO. UP. NO. DOWN.

I'LL COVER MY HAIR. NO. I'LL COVER MY FACE. NO. I'LL COVER MY HAIR AND WEAR SUNGLASSES. NO. GOGGLES. NO. GLASSES. NO. GOGGLES.

NO. I'M RUINING MY SKIN. I'LL JUST SUN MY BACK. NO. MY FRONT. NO. MY SIDE. NO. MY BACK. NO. MY FRONT.

WHY IS YOUR TAN ALWAYS SO EVEN AND MINE'S ALL BLOTCHY?

CATHY'S COMING FOR DINNER. IF I FIX SOMETHING FATTENING, SHE'LL THINK I'M INSENSITIVE TO HER DIET.

IF I FIX A DIET MEAL, SHE'LL THINK I'M TELLING HER SHE NEEDS TO LOSE WEIGHT.

IF I FIX A MEAL THAT COULD GO EITHER WAY, SHE'LL TAKE IT WRONG, BOTH WAYS.

HI, CATHY. YOUR MOTHER'S MAKING HER SPECIALTY.

FILET OF PARANOIA.

WE'LL HAVE THE BABY BAY SHRIMP AND BABY HEARTS-OF-PALM SALAD TO START.

THEN WE'D LIKE THE YOUNG CHICKEN ENTRÉE WITH TEENY NEW POTATOES AND BABY SQUASH.

DOES THAT COME WITH THOSE CUTE LITTLE BABY CARROTS?

OH, AND WE WANT THE EENSY-BEANSY BABY CORN-ON-THE-COBS...

AND THE TEENSY ADORABLE BABY ASPARAGUS.

THIS IS AS CLOSE TO PARENTING AS EITHER OF US EXPECTS TO GET FOR A WHILE.

SHE'S HOLDING AN INFANT. IF I ASK WHAT SHE DOES FOR A LIVING, SHE'LL BE OFFENDED.

IF SHE **ALSO** GOES TO AN OFFICE EVERY DAY AND I **DON'T** ASK WHAT SHE DOES FOR A LIVING, SHE'LL BE OFFENDED.

IF I AVOID THE WHOLE SUBJECT BY DISCUSSING EVERYTHING EXCEPT HER LIFE, SHE'LL BE OFFENDED.

WHY AREN'T YOU TALKING TO OUR HOSTESS, CATHY?

I CAN'T DECIDE ON THE PROPER WAY TO INSULT HER.

CATHY AND I HAVE REALLY BEEN POWERING OUT AT WORK!

WE USED TO THINK THAT WAS IMPORTANT BEFORE THE BABY.

WE DIDN'T GET TO THE NEW SUSHI PLACE UNTIL THIS WEEK!

WE HAVEN'T BEEN TO A NEW RESTAURANT SINCE THE BABY!

WE HAVE SOMETHING VERY SPECIAL TOGETHER!

WE DIDN'T KNOW THE MEANING OF LOVE UNTIL THE BABY!

I FEEL VERY CLOSE TO YOU, MAX. WE'RE STARTING TO GET REJECTED AS A COUPLE.

QUIET! BABY SLEEPING

5:45... THANK HEAVENS. IN 15 MINUTES I CAN RUSH TO MY HEALTH CLUB AND START PUSHING GIANT MACHINES AROUND THAT I MAKE HEAVIER ON PURPOSE.

IF I HURRY I CAN EVEN SPEND 30 MINUTES TORTURING MY MUSCLES IN A SWEATY ROOM WHILE SOMEONE SCREAMS AT ME OVER PUNK ROCK LOVE SONGS.

EVERY YEAR THIS DESK MAKES SOMETHING WORSE SEEM LIKE FUN.

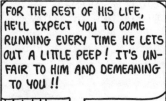

SEEING ALL OUR FRIENDS WITH BABIES IS REALLY GETTING TO ME, CATHY.

I'M STARTING TO THINK MAYBE ALL THIS ISN'T ENOUGH... MAYBE I'M MISSING SOMETHING SPECIAL.

THERE'S A BIG EMPTY SPOT IN ONE OF THE MOST IMPORTANT PLACES IN MY LIFE.

OH, SWEETIE...

I WANT A GERRY CAR-SEAT IN MY BMW !!!

PASS THE PERRIER, MAX.

MAX HAS EVERY TOY A MAN CAN BUY WITHOUT HAVING A CHILD TO RATIONALIZE IT ON...

...PHONES, COMPUTERS, MONITORS, SPEAKERS, SCREENS, PRINTERS, PLAYERS, HUNDREDS OF ELECTRONIC GIZMOS...

NOW HE'S SUDDENLY STARTING TO TALK ABOUT WANTING A BABY.

MAX WANTS A BABY?

MEN DON'T HAVE BIOLOGICAL CLOCKS. THEY HAVE BIOLOGICAL UNDERWATER WATCHES.

"GUESS" JEANS FOR INFANTS... EVENING CLOTHES FOR TODDLERS... DESIGNER DIAPERS... $500 STROLLERS... COMPUTERIZED CRIB TOYS....

EVERYWHERE I LOOK, IT'S BABY, BABY, BABY, BABY.

BABY CHIC

FACE IT, CHARLENE. OUR GENERATION HAS FINALLY AWAKENED TO OUR MOST PRIMAL INSTINCTS.

YEAH.

THE NEED TO SHOP.

Panel 1: THESE SUITS ARE AS BAD AS LAST YEAR'S! / OH, NO. THESE ARE **MUCH WORSE!** THEY TOOK THE HIGH-CUT LEGS YOU HATED LAST YEAR AND CUT THEM **HIGHER!**

Panel 2: THEY TOOK THE SKIMPY, SQUASHY NECKLINES THAT INSULTED EVERY FIGURE AND MADE THEM SKIMPIER AND SQUASHIER!

Panel 3: AND ON MANY STYLES THEY ADDED A BELT, SO THE FLAB CAN BULGE OUT BOTH ABOVE AND BELOW THE WAIST!

Panel 4: EVERY CUSTOMER I DRIVE AWAY IS 200 LITTLE PLASTIC HANGERS I DON'T HAVE TO DEAL WITH.

Panel 5: OH, HAH! THIS MUST BE A JOKE! IS THIS A JOKE??

Panel 6: NO ONE COULD LOOK GOOD IN THIS BATHING SUIT! THIS SUIT WAS DESIGNED BY A MANIACAL LUNATIC!

Panel 7: THIS REPULSIVE SCRAP OF POLYESTER IS AN INSULT TO THE HUMAN FORM!!

Panel 8: DID YOU WANT TO TRY THAT ON? / YES.

Panel 9: YOU STILL LOOK FOR BATHING SUITS LIKE YOU LOOK FOR BOYFRIENDS, CATHY.

Panel 10: YOU TOTALLY IGNORE THE ONES THAT MAKE SENSE AND INSIST ON FRUSTRATING YOURSELF WITH THE DAZZLING BUT IMPOSSIBLE ONES.

Panel 11: THERE... SEE?? WHY WOULD YOU EVEN **TRY** A SUIT SHAPED LIKE THAT?! / IT'S MY LAST GASP OF YOUTH, ANDREA.

Panel 12: I'D RATHER LOOK BAD IN A CONVERTIBLE THAN NICE IN A STATION WAGON.